Psychic Dogs

Journeys Beyond the Leash

Lee Brickley

Copyright @ Lee Brickley 2023

Chapters

Introduction..5

Echoes in Edinburgh...11

Birmingham's Barking Seer...17

The Whispering Welsh Corgi...23

Boston's Beacon...29

The Guardian of Greenwich...35

Liverpool's Luminescent Labrador..41

Mysteries in Manchester..47

The Texan Tail-Teller...53

New Orleans' Nocturnal Nudger..59

Savannah's Sensing Spaniel...65

California's Canine Clairvoyant...71

Glasgow's Greyhound..77

Seattle's Sorrow-Sensing Setter...83

Apparitions and the Appalachian Akita....................................89

The Prophetic Pup of Portsmouth...95

Denver's Dreaming Dalmatian..101

London's Lassie..107

The Boxer of San Francisco..113

Miami's Mourning Maltese...119

Newcastle's Nighttime Navigator...125

The Phantom Feeler of Philadelphia...131

Tales of a Tucson Terrier..137

Virginia's Visionary Vizsla..143

The West Midlands Whippet..149

Afterword..155

About The Author..161

Introduction

In the dimly lit corners of our world, where shadows seem to whisper and the wind carries tales of the long-forgotten, our lives intersect with the inexplicable. I am Lee Brickley, a paranormal investigator, and throughout my many ventures into the eerie unknown, I have encountered phenomena that both defy logic and awaken an ancient curiosity nestled within our souls. But in all my experiences, none have been as intriguing, or as profoundly personal, as the tales I've unearthed about our most loyal companions: dogs.

They've been by our side for thousands of years, protective guardians and loving friends, their lives entwined with ours in an age-old dance of trust and affection. The bond between a person and their dog is unlike any other—deeply emotional, intuitively connected. It's no surprise, then, that amidst the numerous accounts of the paranormal I've stumbled upon, a significant number have dogs at their centre. "Psychic Dogs: Journeys Beyond the Leash" is an exploration of these uncanny tales that tiptoe the line between the familiar warmth of our beloved pets and the chilling unknown.

Every culture, every age has stories of spectral apparitions and premonitions. Often, these tales are brushed off as mere coincidences or overactive imaginations. Yet, as I delved deeper, a pattern emerged—a consistent thread of dogs demonstrating an uncanny awareness of events beyond human comprehension. Were these simply random acts of canine intuition, or could there be more to our furry friends than meets the eye?

Throughout this book, you will read tales from the bustling streets of London to the vast expanses of Texas—stories that will send shivers down your spine, make you question the boundaries of our reality, and, paradoxically, warm your heart. These tales aren't just about dogs with an uncanny ability to predict, sense, or communicate; they're about the strength and depth of the bond between a dog and its human. And it's within this bond that the paranormal finds a playground.

So, you might ask, can dogs truly be psychic? Well, the world of the paranormal is built on experiences more than proofs. It thrives on the anecdotes of those who've felt a ghostly chill, seen an apparition, or in this case, observed their four-legged friend react to something unseeable. While many of us cherish our pets for their loyalty, love, and playfulness, there are those who have found an additional layer to their bond—a layer that dances on the edge of the ethereal.

Now, you might be glancing at your own canine companion, perhaps resting by your feet or gazing at you with those soulful eyes, and wondering, "Could my dog be psychic?" While there's no litmus test for psychic ability (in humans or dogs), there are certain signs you can look out for.

Dogs are creatures of habit, but if you find your pet displaying consistent behaviours before specific events (be it a sudden bark minutes before a phone rings or a restless pacing before a storm), it might be more than mere coincidence. Some dogs have shown sensitivity to places with reported paranormal activity, acting nervous, or refusing to enter certain areas. Others may demonstrate an unusual attachment to a specific object or picture, particularly if it belonged to someone who has passed away. Their heightened senses might pick up on subtle energies or shifts that we, in our human limitations, might miss.

It's also worth noting your dog's reactions to new people or situations. While most dogs might bark at a stranger, if your pet displays a consistent, inexplicable aversion to certain individuals or places, it might be worth considering that they're picking up on something not immediately apparent to you.

However, it's essential to approach such observations with a balanced perspective. Before jumping to supernatural conclusions, always consider the rational explanations. A dog's acute senses—particularly hearing and smell—can pick up on things that might escape human notice. The key is consistency and patterns in behaviour. If your pet demonstrates repeated actions that cannot be explained through everyday stimuli, you might just have a psychic pooch on your hands.

Delving into these tales, I encourage readers to approach with an open heart and mind. Whether you're a steadfast believer in the paranormal or a loving dog owner who's witnessed your pet do something inexplicably extraordinary, this book is a journey. A journey into the heart of mystery, into the profound bond between humans and dogs, and into the vast, shadowy realm of the unknown.

As we navigate through these tales, remember, the veil between our world and the mystical is thin and ever-shifting. And sometimes, our most loyal companions, with their unyielding trust and keen senses, might just be our best guides through the enigma. So, dear reader, as you turn these pages, may you feel the soft padding of paws beside you, hear the gentle whisper of the unknown, and see the world through the wondrous eyes of our psychic dogs.

And in those silent moments, in the depth of night when the world is hushed, look to your faithful friend. For in their eyes might lie mysteries waiting to be uncovered, tales of the past, present, and perhaps even the future.

Welcome to "Psychic Dogs: Journeys Beyond the Leash." Your adventure into the enigmatic realm of paranormal paws begins now.

Echoes in Edinburgh

Edinburgh, with its cobbled streets and historic buildings, holds tales as ancient as the stones that pave its roads. Every nook and cranny of this Scottish city whispers stories of battles, monarchs, and mysteries. But the tale I'm about to share is not about a king or a war—it's about a small Scottish Terrier named Angus.

Angus was the pride and joy of Eleanor, a retired school teacher who had spent her entire life in the heart of Edinburgh. A sprightly old woman with a sparkle in her eye and a love for history, Eleanor often regaled her neighbours with tales of the city's past. Angus, with his jet-black fur and a pert little nose, was always at her side, listening intently, or so it seemed.

One chilly evening, as the fog rolled in from the North Sea, cloaking the city in a dense mist, Eleanor settled into her armchair with a cup of tea. As she took a sip, she heard Angus growling softly, his gaze fixed on the fireplace. Eleanor followed his gaze, but saw nothing out of the ordinary. "What is it, boy?" she asked, reaching out to pet him. But Angus's attention didn't waver.

Eleanor tried to brush it off, thinking perhaps a draft had caused the flames to flicker or dance, catching Angus's attention. Yet, every evening thereafter, like clockwork, Angus would growl at the fireplace, his tiny body tense, his eyes wide.

It was on one such evening, with the wind howling outside and rain lashing against the windows, that Eleanor heard it—a faint whisper, almost drowned out by the storm. Straining her ears, she made out the words: "Help...find me..." The voice seemed to be coming from the very fireplace Angus was so fixated on.

Heart pounding, Eleanor approached the hearth. The voice grew louder, clearer, its desperate plea echoing in her ears.

Angus, too, seemed to respond to the voice, whimpering and pacing around the room.

Now, most would dismiss such an event as the wind playing tricks or perhaps the onset of age-related hallucinations. But Eleanor, with her knowledge of Edinburgh's history, had a different theory. She remembered tales of secret tunnels and hidden rooms in some of the city's oldest homes—spaces that had been sealed off and forgotten. Could her home, passed down through generations, hold such a secret?

With newfound determination, Eleanor began her research. She scoured old property records, maps, and architectural drawings. Late one night, she stumbled upon an ancient blueprint of her home, revealing a hidden chamber behind the fireplace. Her heart raced. The whispers, Angus's reactions—they all made sense now.

Armed with this knowledge, Eleanor contacted an expert to explore and possibly excavate the fireplace. As the bricks were carefully removed, a small, concealed space revealed itself. It was a tiny room, with remnants of old furniture and personal effects. The most striking find, however, was a small locket containing a portrait of a young woman, her face eerily familiar.

Eleanor felt a shiver run down her spine. She recognized the woman from old family portraits—she was an ancestor who had disappeared without a trace, her fate a mystery that had haunted the family for generations.

As the room was further explored, they discovered a diary. It belonged to the young woman, Isabella, and its pages told a tragic tale. Isabella had fallen in love with a man her family disapproved of. In their attempt to keep them apart, Isabella was confined to this hidden chamber, her pleas and cries unheard, her existence erased.

Eleanor, moved by the heart-wrenching story, decided to give Isabella the recognition and peace she had been denied in life. With the help of historians and experts, she brought Isabella's story to light, organising an exhibit in her honour.

From that day, the whispers ceased. Angus no longer growled at the fireplace. Instead, every so often, Eleanor would find him wagging his tail, looking at a spot just above the hearth, as if someone was there, petting him. Eleanor liked to believe that it was Isabella, finally free and at peace, showing her gratitude.

This tale, one among many in my collection, reinforces the belief that animals, especially dogs, have a heightened sensitivity, an ability to perceive things beyond our understanding. Angus, with his unwavering focus on the fireplace, served as a bridge between the past and the present, between the living and the spirits. His connection to the paranormal not only unravelled a century-old mystery but also brought solace to a lost soul.

In the heart of Edinburgh, amidst tales of kings and battles, the legend of a small Scottish Terrier and a forgotten ancestor finds its place, reminding us that sometimes, the most profound stories are not of wars or monarchs but of love, loyalty, and the bonds that transcend time.

Birmingham's Barking Seer

Birmingham, a melting pot of culture and history, has long been home to tales of innovation and progress. From its bustling markets to its iconic factories, the city has always pulsed with a distinct energy. But in the midst of its urban tales, there's one that stands out not because of its grandeur but because of its uncanny nature—a tale revolving around an English Bulldog named Winston.

James Thompson, a mechanical engineer, had always been a man of logic and precision. His life revolved around blueprints, calculations, and machines. Little did he know that his life would take an unexpected turn when he decided to adopt a stocky, wrinkled-faced English Bulldog from a local shelter.

Named after the iconic Winston Churchill, owing to his

determined gait and a somewhat grumpy expression, the dog quickly became an integral part of the Thompson household. The family was smitten with his antics—from his comical efforts to catch his tail to his absolute refusal to move during rain.

It was during one of Birmingham's infamous drizzles that Mrs. Thompson noticed something peculiar. Every time a family member was about to visit, Winston would position himself by the window, staring intently at a particular corner, sometimes hours before their arrival. Initially dismissed as coincidence, this behaviour soon became too consistent to ignore.

But Winston's foresight wasn't limited to predicting visits. One summer afternoon, as Mrs. Thompson prepared tea, she heard a distressed bark coming from the living room. Rushing in, she found Winston staring at a family portrait, his whines growing more frantic. Hours later, they received a call that James's elderly mother, pictured in that very portrait, had been taken ill.

As days turned into weeks and weeks into months, the Thompsons began to notice a pattern. Whenever a family event—be it joyous or unfortunate—was on the horizon, Winston would display distinct behaviours. A circle around the dining table signified a family gathering, a low growl by the phone indicated bad news, and a jubilant dance with his favourite toy foreshadowed celebrations.

Word quickly spread around the neighbourhood about Birmingham's barking seer. Curious neighbours, initially sceptical, became believers after witnessing Winston's predictions firsthand. Some even claimed that Winston would bark in a distinct pattern days before the local football team had a win.

Naturally, such phenomena caught the attention of local media. Reporters and journalists frequented the Thompson residence, all keen to document Winston's next prediction. Animal behaviourists also took an interest, attempting to decipher the mystery behind the bulldog's uncanny abilities.

Multiple theories arose. Some attributed it to heightened senses, suggesting that Winston could perceive subtle changes in the environment or even in human physiology that indicated upcoming events. Others leaned towards the paranormal, hinting at a deeper, mystical connection between Winston and the world around him.

For James Thompson, a man grounded in logic and science, accepting that his dog had some form of psychic ability was challenging. Yet, even he couldn't dismiss the mounting evidence. Each prediction, each accurate foreshadowing, chipped away at his scepticism.

The most poignant moment came on a cold December evening. As snowflakes painted Birmingham white, the Thompsons settled by the fireplace, the warmth contrasting the icy world outside. Suddenly, Winston began a low, melancholic howl, his eyes fixated on James. The family watched in silence, an uneasy feeling settling in their hearts.

Hours later, in the dead of night, James experienced a heart ailment. Thanks to Winston's warning, the family was alert and quickly sought medical help, saving James's life.

In the days that followed, as James recuperated, he reflected upon the incredible events of the past months. Winston, with his inexplicable abilities, had not only predicted numerous family events but had also saved his life. The bulldog, in his own unique way, had blurred the lines between logic and mysticism for James.

As years passed, the tales of Winston's predictions became legendary in Birmingham. The bulldog, with his droopy eyes and saggy skin, had etched a permanent mark in the annals of the city's lore. Families across the region began to look at their pets with renewed curiosity, wondering if their furry companions, too, held mysterious abilities.

Winston's legacy, however, was not just his psychic prowess. It was the profound impact he had on the Thompsons and the larger community. He embodied the enigmatic bond between humans and their pets—a bond that, at times, transcends understanding, challenging our beliefs and perceptions.

In the heart of Birmingham, amidst tales of industry and progress, Winston's story serves as a gentle reminder that life's mysteries are not always found in grand events or historic milestones. Sometimes, they're nestled in the everyday moments, in the wag of a tail, the bark of a dog, or the silent, knowing gaze of our loyal companions.

For in those moments, if we look close enough, we might just find a hint of the magic that threads our world, waiting to be discovered, cherished, and passed down through generations.

The Whispering Welsh Corgi

Wales, with its rolling green hills, ancient castles, and a rich tapestry of myths and legends, has always been a land of enchantment. In the quaint town of Llandudno, nestled between the Irish Sea and the peaks of Snowdonia, a new legend was taking shape—one centred around a humble Welsh Corgi named Bran.

The Davies family had lived in Llandudno for generations. Their home, a cosy stone cottage, was as much a part of the town's history as the Great Orme or the Victorian pier. The Davies were known for their sheep farming, and over the years, they had a variety of herding dogs. But Bran was different.

With his short legs, expressive eyes, and a coat that shimmered like a moonlit night, Bran captivated anyone who laid eyes on him. But it wasn't his appearance that set him apart; it was something more ethereal.

The first inkling of Bran's unique nature became evident shortly after Mr. Davies brought him home. It was during the harsh winter months, with snowstorms often blanketing the town. On a particularly chilly evening, as Mrs. Davies was setting the dinner table, Bran began to whimper and paw at the door that led to the barn.

Thinking he might need to go outside, Mrs. Davies opened the door, but instead of dashing out, Bran sat down, refusing to budge, his gaze fixed on the barn. Sensing his distress, Mr. Davies decided to inspect the barn. To his horror, he discovered that a faulty heater had sparked a small fire, threatening to engulf the structure and the livestock inside. Thanks to Bran's timely warning, a major catastrophe was averted.

Word of the incident spread through Llandudno like wildfire. But this was just the beginning of Bran's mysterious deeds.

Months later, as spring painted the town in vibrant hues, the Davies planned a trip to the nearby Conwy Castle. The morning of the trip, as they were packing the car, Bran became unusually restless. He kept darting between Mrs. Davies and the car, barking insistently. Every attempt to get him inside the vehicle was met with resistance. Eventually, the family, albeit reluctantly, decided to postpone the trip.

Later that day, they learned that a massive landslide had blocked the route to the castle. Had they set out as planned, they would've been caught in it.

These incidents were not mere coincidences. Time and again, Bran displayed an uncanny ability to sense impending misfortunes. When a storm was brewing, even if the skies were clear, Bran would herd the family's sheep to the safety of the barn. If any family member was about to make a decision that would lead to trouble, Bran would act agitated, sometimes even placing himself as a barrier to stop them.

The townsfolk of Llandudno, while no strangers to tales of

magic and mystique, were both baffled and awed by Bran's abilities. Some believed he was a guardian spirit, reincarnated to protect the Davies. Others thought he had inherited the ancient energies of the land.

For young Eira Davies, Bran was more than just a mystical protector; he was her best friend. The bond they shared was palpable. Bran seemed especially attuned to Eira's emotions. If she was upset or in distress, he'd be by her side, offering silent comfort. This connection between them played a crucial role in what came to be known as the most astonishing incident of all.

It was late autumn, and Eira, now a curious ten-year-old, decided to explore the caves near the Great Orme with her friends. As the group ventured deeper into the labyrinthine tunnels, they lost track of time and direction.

Back home, as dusk approached, Bran became visibly anxious. He paced around, his barks growing more frantic. Sensing that Eira was in trouble, he bolted out of the house and towards the Great Orme.

Inside the cave, as darkness enveloped the tunnels, Eira and her friends began to panic. Their shouts for help echoed, but there was no one around to hear them. Just when hope was dwindling, they heard a familiar bark. Following the sound, they were led out of the cave by Bran, who had managed to pinpoint their location.

The town hailed Bran as a hero. Eira's rescue cemented his status as the "Whispering Welsh Corgi," a guardian whose whispers resonated not through words, but through actions, guiding his family away from harm.

As years rolled on, the tales of Bran's deeds grew. They became a testament to the deep, mystical bond that can exist between humans and their pets—a bond that is sometimes woven with threads of the unknown.

In the shadow of Snowdonia, amidst tales of dragons and knights, Bran's story found its place. Not as a grand epic, but as a gentle reminder that sometimes, magic is found in the wag of a tail, the nuzzle of a snout, or the unwavering gaze of a loyal companion who, in his own way, whispers the ancient secrets of the land.

Boston's Beacon

Amidst the historic streets of Boston, where every brick and cobblestone whispers tales of revolutions and legacies, a modern-day story was unfolding. A story that interwove the intricate threads of medical marvel with the inexplicable bonds of the heart. At the centre of this narrative was an ordinary Beagle named Charlie and his owner, Sarah Mitchell.

Sarah, a young graphic designer, had moved to Boston for a fresh start. The city, with its blend of old-world charm and new-age dynamism, seemed like the perfect canvas for her aspirations. However, there was one shadow that loomed over her dreams: epilepsy. Diagnosed in her late teens, Sarah grappled with the unpredictability of seizures. The episodes were sporadic, with little warning, making everyday activities a challenge.

On a recommendation, Sarah decided to adopt a pet, hoping the companionship would provide some solace. Enter Charlie—a playful Beagle with an insatiable curiosity. From the moment Sarah laid eyes on him at the rescue centre, there was an unmistakable connection. His warm brown eyes mirrored a depth of understanding that belied his playful antics.

The duo quickly became inseparable. Morning walks along the Charles River, brunches in North End cafes, and leisurely strolls through Boston Common became their shared rituals. In Charlie, Sarah found not just a pet, but a confidante, a partner in crime, and a beacon of hope.

A few months into their partnership, on a particularly stormy night, as thunder rumbled and lightning streaked the sky, Sarah felt the familiar and dreaded aura of an impending seizure. Alone in her apartment, fear gripped her. But Charlie, sensing her distress, immediately sprang into action. He climbed onto her lap, pressing his body against hers, his steady heartbeat a counter-rhythm to her escalating panic.

What happened next was nothing short of miraculous. Instead of succumbing to a full-blown seizure, Sarah's symptoms began to subside. Charlie's presence, his warmth, seemed to act as a stabilising force, grounding her.

Encouraged by this incident, Sarah began to notice a pattern. Whenever a seizure threatened to take hold, Charlie would alert her. Sometimes through a persistent bark, other times by nudging her or pacing restlessly. This early warning system gave Sarah precious minutes to prepare—either by taking medication, moving to a safer location, or alerting someone.

Word of Charlie's unique ability spread amongst Sarah's friends and colleagues. Many were amazed, some sceptical. But for Sarah, the proof was in the lived experience. Time and again, Charlie had come to her aid, his intuitive sense acting as a beacon, guiding her through the tumultuous waters of epilepsy.

Intrigued by this phenomenon, Sarah decided to collaborate with a local research institute, hoping to understand the mechanics behind Charlie's ability. Over weeks, the duo underwent a series of tests and observations.

The findings were enlightening. Researchers hypothesise that Charlie, with his heightened olfactory senses, could detect minute changes in Sarah's biochemistry—changes that signalled the onset of a seizure. Additionally, his keen observational skills allowed him to pick up on subtle behavioural cues that even Sarah wasn't consciously aware of.

But science aside, what stood out was the profound bond between Sarah and Charlie. It was this bond, this deep connection, that amplified Charlie's natural instincts, turning him from a mere pet to a life-saving companion.

The story of "Boston's Beacon" resonated far and wide. Local newspapers featured them, and soon, national platforms picked up their tale. Through interviews and appearances, Sarah and Charlie managed to shed light on both the challenges of living with epilepsy and the incredible potential of service dogs.

However, for Sarah, the media attention was secondary. What mattered most was the renewed sense of autonomy and confidence that Charlie brought into her life. No longer did she view her condition as a debilitating limitation. Instead, with Charlie by her side, she felt empowered to take on the world.

Their adventures continued—exploring Boston's historic landmarks, savouring its culinary delights, and delving into its vibrant arts scene. Each day was a testament to their partnership, a dance of mutual trust and understanding.

In the heart of Boston, a city known for its pioneering spirit and revolutionary tales, Sarah and Charlie carved out their own legacy. A story that transcended the boundaries of human and animal, proving that sometimes, our greatest allies come in the form of four-legged friends. Friends who, with their unwavering loyalty and keen instincts, illuminate our paths, ensuring we never walk alone in the dark.

The Guardian of Greenwich

Greenwich, with its serene maritime charm, was a haven for families seeking a quiet retreat from the bustling life of nearby London. Among its quaint Victorian houses and winding lanes, the tale of Lucas, a gleaming Golden Retriever, and the Harvey family unfurled—a tale that melded the borders of reality and dreams.

The Harveys were a tight-knit family. Helen, a schoolteacher, her husband Paul, an architect, and their two children, Isabelle and Jake, lived a life of predictable comforts. But there was one void, one whisper of the past that often echoed in their home—the mysterious disappearance of Helen's elder brother, Daniel, over a decade ago. As years wore on, memories of Daniel had faded into old photographs and seldom-spoken words.

Into this backdrop, Lucas entered as a beacon of golden light. With his warm, russet eyes, and a tail that wagged like a metronome, he brought an infectious joy. Lucas was especially attached to Helen, often shadowing her around the house, lying by her feet, or nuzzling her when she was down.

One fateful evening, after a particularly exhausting day at work, Helen drifted into a deep sleep on the living room couch. As the golden hues of the setting sun streamed through the window, she found herself in a dream—a vivid tapestry of colours and sounds that felt almost tangible.

She stood by the riverside in Greenwich, the gentle hum of the water and the distant toll of the ship's bell filling the air. There, amidst the familiar setting, she saw a figure she hadn't seen in over a decade—Daniel. He looked just as she remembered, his face etched with the lines of wisdom that time bestows. They spoke, not through words, but through a deep, soulful connection, reminiscing about their shared past and the moments lost in time.

When Helen awoke, the weight of the dream bore down on her. She could recall every detail—the warmth of Daniel's smile, the soft timbre of his laughter, the scent of the river. But what struck her most was Lucas, who lay beside her, watching her intently, his gaze almost understanding.

The dreams continued. Night after night, Helen found herself reuniting with Daniel, traversing the landscapes of their shared memories. And every morning, she'd find Lucas beside her, as if he'd journeyed with her, bridging the realms of consciousness and dreams.

Curiosity led to exploration. Helen began maintaining a journal, documenting each dream in meticulous detail. Patterns emerged. Many dreams centred around specific places in Greenwich—places of significance to Daniel and Helen's shared history. The old bookstore where they'd spent countless hours, the ice cream parlour that heralded their summer adventures, the pier where they'd whispered secrets into the night.

One evening, as Helen recounted a particularly poignant

dream to Paul, Isabelle, and Jake, an idea took root. What if they revisited these places? Could there be clues, tangible remnants of the past, waiting to be discovered?

With Lucas leading the way, the Harveys embarked on this unique pilgrimage. At every location, Lucas displayed an uncanny recognition. He'd sniff around, sometimes barking joyfully, other times whining softly. Each reaction seemed to mirror the emotional tone of Helen's dreams.

As weeks turned into months, the excursions became a healing journey for the Harveys. While they didn't find any concrete clues about Daniel's whereabouts, they discovered something even more profound—closure. The dreams and Lucas's reactions helped Helen process her grief and guilt, allowing her to cherish the memories without being shackled by the pain of loss.

It was during a visit to their childhood home, now an old, weathered structure, that the final piece of the puzzle fell into place. Lucas, after a frenzied bout of sniffing, led the family to the backyard. There, buried under the old oak tree, was a small metal box—a time capsule that Helen and Daniel had buried as children. Inside were trinkets of their childhood—marbles, postcards, a toy soldier, and a letter.

The letter, written in Daniel's neat handwriting, was a message to their future selves. It spoke of hopes and dreams, of the bond they shared, and a promise that no matter where life took them, they'd always find their way back to each other.

As Helen read the letter aloud, tears streaming down her face, Lucas nuzzled her, offering silent comfort. In that moment, the Harveys felt Daniel's presence, not as a haunting spectre of the past but as a warm, comforting embrace.

The Guardian of Greenwich, as Lucas became fondly known, had done more than any detective or search party. He'd reconnected a family with their lost loved one, not through maps or clues, but through the ethereal world of dreams.

The tale of Lucas and the Harveys became a heartwarming

legend in Greenwich. It served as a testament to the mysterious, intangible bonds that tie us, proving that love and memories, when guided by forces beyond our comprehension, have the power to transcend the barriers of time and space.

Liverpool's Luminescent Labrador

Liverpool, the city of the Beatles, football, and maritime tales, has always been awash with stories of history and hauntings. But amidst its urban legends and dockside ballads, the story of a Labrador named Nero stands distinct, blending the everyday with the eerily extraordinary.

The Davidson family, consisting of James, an academic at the University of Liverpool, his wife Lila, a pediatric nurse, and their teenage daughter Anna, resided in a classic red-brick terraced house, a stone's throw away from the iconic Albert Dock. Their lives were as ordinary as the next family, with routines, small joys, and the occasional squabble. That is, until Nero came bounding into their lives, a bundle of black fur with a white star-shaped patch on his chest.

Nero was an exuberant pup, bringing the typical Labrador chaos—chewed shoes, knocked-over vases, and endless games of fetch. However, as weeks turned into months, the Davidsons began noticing something atypical about their pet.

The first incident was subtle. Anna was up late, engrossed in a novel, with Nero sprawled at her feet. As midnight approached, she felt a draft, despite all windows being closed. The lights flickered momentarily. Looking down, Anna caught a faint glow emanating from Nero. It was subtle, a soft luminescence outlining his silhouette, casting a gentle light on the pages of her book. Before she could process it, the glow faded, and everything returned to normal.

Thinking it was a trick of her tired eyes, Anna brushed it off. But soon, other family members started experiencing similar occurrences.

Lila was in the kitchen one evening when she felt a sudden

drop in temperature. As she rubbed her arms to ward off the chill, she saw Nero, sitting by the pantry, glowing with a soft, ethereal light. This time, the glow was more pronounced, illuminating the entire room in a pale blue hue. Nero seemed calm, almost contemplative, his eyes fixed on a spot near the pantry. And then, as quickly as it began, the glow subsided, and Nero trotted over to Lila, tail wagging, as if nothing out of the ordinary had occurred.

Baffled, James, being a man of science, decided to investigate. He began by observing Nero, documenting each glowing incident. He noticed a pattern. The luminescence wasn't random—it seemed to coincide with small, inexplicable phenomena in the house. A sudden cold draft, despite no open windows. The sound of footsteps when no one else was home. The fleeting scent of roses in the middle of winter.

The Davidsons, though initially startled, began to view Nero's glow as a protective shield, a beacon that seemed to ward off these mysterious occurrences. Whenever the glow appeared, the eerie disturbances would subside, replaced by a comforting warmth and calm.

Curious about the history of their home, James delved into local archives. He discovered that their house, built in the early 19th century, had been inhabited by a sea captain named Arthur and his wife Eliza. Tragically, Arthur had perished at sea, leaving Eliza heartbroken. She spent her remaining years in the house, waiting for her husband's return. It was said that she would light a candle every night, placing it by the window, a beacon for her lost love.

Connecting the dots, the Davidsons theorised that the mysterious occurrences might be remnants of Eliza's lingering presence, her eternal wait symbolised by the fleeting phenomena. And Nero, with his unexplained luminescence, seemed to be the modern-day equivalent of Eliza's candle, a beacon in the shadows.

Anna, with her love for stories, often sat with Nero during these glowing moments, whispering tales of the sea, of lost love, and of hope, as if to comfort the lingering spirit of Eliza. With each story, the disturbances in the house grew less frequent, replaced by a palpable sense of peace.

Over time, Nero's luminescence became less frequent. The house, once filled with mysterious drafts and unexplained sounds, settled into an unspoken tranquillity. The Davidsons believed that their love, their acceptance, and Nero's mysterious glow had somehow bridged the chasm between the past and the present, allowing Eliza's spirit to finally find the solace she had been seeking.

Nero lived a long, happy life with the Davidsons. His luminescence, though rarer in his later years, never ceased to amaze and comfort the family. He wasn't just a pet; he was their guardian, their luminescent Labrador, guiding them through moments of uncertainty with his gentle, glowing light.

The tale of Nero became a cherished family legend, passed down through generations. For the Davidsons, it was a testament to the unexplained wonders of the world, the thin veil separating the tangible from the ethereal, and the profound bonds that can form between humans and their canine companions, bonds that shine, even in the darkest of nights.

Mysteries in Manchester

Manchester, a bustling metropolis known for its industrial heritage, football clubs, and vibrant arts scene, is also home to a myriad of stories, each corner echoing with tales of the city's rich history. One such story emerges from the cobbled streets of the Ancoats neighbourhood, tucked away in one of the old Victorian terraces where the Cartwright family resided.

Ruth Cartwright, a historian at the University of Manchester, lived with her two children, Sam and Eliza, and her elderly mother, Mrs. Clara Benson. The household was completed by their elegant and rather astute poodle, Marcel. With his silver-grey curls and sharp, observant eyes, Marcel was more than just a pet; he was an integral part of the family. And as the Cartwrights soon found out, he had an uncanny knack for uncovering the past.

The house had been in the Benson family for generations, passed down from one era to the next, its walls seeped in family lore. Clara often regaled her grandchildren with tales of their ancestors — stories of wartime heroes, celebrated artists, and shrewd business tycoons. And accompanying these tales were whispers of hidden family heirlooms, passed down but lost to the annals of time. Clara, in her old age, often spoke of a particular heirloom — a locket that had once belonged to her great-grandmother. Despite its monetary worth being negligible, its sentimental value was unparalleled. Sadly, the whereabouts of the locket remained a mystery, assumed to be lost or sold by previous generations.

It was on a damp, drizzly afternoon that Marcel's mysterious talent first came to light. Eliza and Sam were playing hide and seek, with Marcel eagerly joining the fun. As Eliza hid behind an old wardrobe in the attic, she noticed Marcel intently scratching at a section of the wooden floorboards. Curious, she called her brother, and together they pried open the loosened board to reveal a dusty, old tin box. Inside, wrapped in brittle paper, was the long-lost locket, its golden chain intertwined with a handwritten note.

Ecstatic, the children rushed to show their discovery to Clara. The elderly woman, with tears in her eyes, clasped the locket, whispering words of gratitude and love. The note, dated from the late 1800s, was from Clara's great-grandfather to her great-grandmother, expressing his undying affection and hope that the locket would be passed down as a symbol of their everlasting love.

The family was stunned. How had Marcel known? It was a question that lingered in the air, but the intrigue didn't end there.

Over the following months, Marcel displayed an inexplicable affinity for uncovering hidden nooks and crannies in the house. Beneath the staircase, he sniffed out a collection of old coins from various eras, stashed away by a globe-trotting ancestor. Behind a loose brick in the fireplace, Marcel discovered a stash of wartime letters, filled with tales of bravery and longing, exchanged between

Clara's grandparents.

With each discovery, the family grew more enamoured with their mysterious poodle. Ruth, ever the historian, began documenting Marcel's finds, drawing connections between the heirlooms and her family tree, unravelling tales that had long been buried.

One evening, as Ruth was engrossed in her research, Marcel began pawing at an old portrait of a stern-looking gentleman — Clara's great-great-uncle, a reputed businessman in Manchester. Upon closer inspection, Ruth discovered a hidden compartment behind the portrait. Inside was a diary, detailing the gentleman's travels, business dealings, and personal reflections. It was a treasure trove of history, offering insights into Manchester's industrial past and the family's role in shaping it.

As months turned into years, Marcel's finds became less frequent, but his legacy was cemented. The Cartwright house transformed into a living museum, each room echoing with tales of the past, thanks to their intuitive poodle.

The family never truly unravelled the mystery behind Marcel's talent. Was it an uncanny sense of smell, picking up on scents that had been trapped for decades? Or was it something deeper, a bond between the poodle and the house, connecting him to generations long gone? Whatever the reason, Marcel's gift was cherished, drawing the family closer, bridging the gap between the present and the past.

For the Cartwrights, Marcel was more than just a pet; he was a link to their ancestors, a guardian of their legacy. In the heart of Manchester, amidst the noise and hustle, stood a house filled with stories, memories, and a poodle with an extraordinary gift.

The locket, the letters, the diary — each heirloom had its own tale, but woven together, they painted a rich tapestry of a family's journey through time. And at the centre of it all was Marcel, the poodle with a nose for history, reminding the Cartwrights that sometimes, the past isn't buried deep beneath the ground; it's right under our noses, waiting to be rediscovered.

The Texan Tail-Teller

In the sprawling heartland of Texas, where horizons stretch endlessly and where towns are separated by miles of sun-soaked ranch land, stories grow as tall as the tales the locals tell in the cozy corners of diners and coffee shops. Deep in these stretches, in the small town of Laredo, the Dawson family had a peculiar story of their own. The protagonist of this tale wasn't any member of the Dawson family, but rather their faithful Border Collie, Beau.

Beau, with his glossy black and white coat and penetrating eyes, had been a part of the Dawson ranch since he was a pup. He herded cattle, guarded the homestead, and played tirelessly with the Dawson children — young Lucy and Ben. But as time went on, the family started noticing something extraordinary about Beau that had nothing to do with his usual canine duties.

The Dawson home was one of the older ranch-style houses in Laredo. Time seemed to stand still in their abode. One artefact from the past that still occupied a prideful place was an old rotary phone, sitting in its own alcove in the living room. Its ring was loud, jarring, and rare. With the advent of mobile phones, the house line was seldom used, reserved for calls from a few old friends and the rare telemarketer.

It began innocently enough. Lucy first pointed it out. "Mama, have you noticed Beau sits by the old phone just before it rings?" she'd asked one afternoon, her finger twirling a strand of her golden hair.

Mrs. Dawson, a pragmatic woman, dismissed it initially. "He's probably just found a new spot to rest, dear."

But Lucy's observation was astute. Over the next few weeks, it became unmistakably clear. A few moments before the phone would give off its blaring ring, Beau would saunter over from wherever he was in the house, sit attentively by the phone, tail wagging in slow, deliberate strokes. He'd tilt his head, eyes focused on the device, waiting.

Mr. Dawson, ever the curious type, started to conduct little experiments. He'd ask his friends to call the landline at unannounced times. Each time, like clockwork, Beau would take his position by the phone, awaiting its call. It was uncanny, almost eerie.

It wasn't just the predictability but the precision of Beau's actions that bewildered the Dawsons. How could he sense it? Was it an audible tick in the mechanics of the phone? Was it some vibration imperceptible to human senses?

The children, with the boundless imagination only youth can provide, had a variety of theories. Ben believed Beau had some secret communication with the birds outside, who would alert him. Lucy, ever the romantic, thought Beau had a guardian angel who'd nudge him just before the phone rang.

Mr. Dawson's mother, Granny Dawson, had a different

perspective. She'd been living long enough to trust the inexplicable. One evening, over a family dinner, she leaned in and shared her theory. "You know, animals, especially dogs, are more in tune with the energies of the world than we are. Maybe Beau senses some shift in the energy around that phone."

While no explanation seemed to fit perfectly, the phenomenon became a beloved quirk in the Dawson household. Friends visiting would be regaled with the tale, and often they'd witness it firsthand, leaving with a sense of wonder and a story to tell others.

One fateful day, Beau's gift took on a more poignant significance. Mrs. Dawson had been feeling under the weather. She rested in her room, a pallor to her face that worried the family. The doctor was due to call with some test results. As the sun set, casting the living room in a golden hue, Beau took his position by the phone. The family watched, anxiety thick in the air. The ring, when it came, was almost relieving.

The news wasn't great, but it was manageable. Treatment would be required, but recovery chances were high. As Mrs. Dawson processed the information, Beau ambled over, laying his head gently in her lap, offering silent comfort.

The weeks that followed were challenging for the Dawsons. But through the hospital visits, the treatments, and the uncertainty, one constant remained: Beau's uncanny sense. His connection to the phone became symbolic, a beacon of the unexplained wonders of life amidst the trials of reality.

Years later, with Mrs. Dawson healthy and the family thriving, they often looked back on that period with a mix of gratitude and wonder. Beau aged, as all living beings do. His once glossy coat had streaks of grey, his gait a tad slower. But every time the phone rang, he was there, alert and waiting.

When Beau eventually passed, he left behind countless memories of joy, loyalty, and that unexplained marvel. The phone, still in its alcove, became more than just a relic. It was a testament to life's mysteries and the ways they intertwine with our everyday existence.

In Texas, where the land stretches as far as stories do, the tale of the Texan Tail-Teller became a part of local folklore. A story of a Border Collie, an old rotary phone, and the mysteries that make life an endless journey of discovery.

New Orleans' Nocturnal Nudger

Nestled within the storied lanes of New Orleans, where legends of voodoo and ghosts intertwine with the melodies of jazz, there's an almost forgotten tale. Amidst the aftermath of Hurricane Katrina, a story emerged of an elderly woman named Mae Richardson and her perceptive Dachshund, Pippin.

Pippin wasn't just any dog. Since Mae had taken him in as a puppy, the residents of their Lower Ninth Ward neighbourhood had heard murmurs of the Dachshund's unique "abilities." Whispers spread about Pippin barking at empty corners, fixating on things invisible to the human eye, and acting restlessly days before any significant event.

On nights when the wind carried stories from the past through the city's cobblestone streets, Pippin would often tilt his head, as if listening to voices from another realm. Mae always said with a chuckle, "Pippin's got one paw in the spirit world. He hears things we can't."

When news of Hurricane Katrina began to dominate the headlines, many fled the impending storm. Mae, however, chose to stay in her lifelong home. "Storms come and go," she'd say. "We'll hunker down, and Pippin will let me know if things turn sour."

On the eve of the hurricane, an unsettling energy hung in the air. Pippin was restless. He paced, whined, and kept glancing at the front door, his behaviour reminiscent of the days leading up to personal upheavals in Mae's life. It was as if he was picking up on an approaching calamity, a disturbance in the fabric of their world.

That night, as the rain intensified and winds howled, Mae went to bed, holding Pippin close. But Pippin's unease grew. Around midnight, he began to emit a low, mournful howl. It was unlike any sound Mae had heard from him. It wasn't fear or discomfort. It was a warning.

Suddenly, Pippin began nudging Mae, not just a gentle prod, but with an urgency she had never felt before. Startled awake, Mae felt a cold dampness seeping through her mattress. Water had started to fill the house, stealthily, insidiously.

Lurching out of bed, she realised the gravity of the situation. Pippin's whines turned more insistent, and he headed towards the attic. It was as if he knew that the higher ground was their only refuge.

Navigating the rising waters, Mae clung to Pippin as he led the way, his innate sense guiding them through the dark. Once they reached the attic, they found temporary safety atop an old chest.

Hours felt like days. The rain outside, combined with the chilling cries for help, painted a grim picture. Pippin, usually so energetic, remained close, offering warmth and occasional comforting licks. He seemed to sense Mae's despair, looking into her eyes as if communicating hope.

When daylight finally broke, Mae, remembering stories of stranded survivors during floods, scrawled a plea for help on an old sheet, which she hung from the attic window. Pippin stayed by the window, barking periodically, as if communicating with unseen guardians.

Eventually, their cries for help were answered. A boat, directed by the sight of the white flag and Pippin's persistent barking, approached their submerged home.

In the days that followed, the story of Mae and Pippin's miraculous survival spread throughout the re-emerging community. Many said it was Mae's grit, while others whispered of Pippin's psychic connection.

In a city where tales of spirits and omens are intertwined with everyday life, Pippin's extraordinary intuition earned him a legendary status. For Mae, it solidified something she always felt — that her little Dachshund wasn't just a pet, but a beacon, connected to mysteries beyond human understanding.

Savannah's Sensing Spaniel

In the heart of Georgia lies the city of Savannah, a place that carries with it the weight of history, much of it draped in mystery and spiritual intrigue. The oak trees adorned with Spanish moss stand as silent witnesses to tales that have transpired over centuries. For local historian Lucy Thornton, these tales became more personal when she adopted a Spaniel named Benji.

From the outset, Benji wasn't your typical pup. As a rescue, he came to Lucy quiet and reserved. But it was in the backdrop of Savannah's historic streets that Benji's unusual tendencies began to manifest.

Lucy lived near one of Savannah's most iconic squares, which had been the site of numerous tales of hauntings and eerie occurrences. On their evening walks, Benji would frequently stop, ears perked up, tail wagging slowly, staring intently at seemingly empty spaces. On some nights, his gaze would fixate on a particular bench or corner, and he would whine softly, almost melancholically.

Initially, Lucy dismissed these as quirks. But as time went on, the patterns became harder to ignore. She began to notice that Benji's reactions often coincided with locations known for their paranormal activity. The bench he'd often stop at? It was said to be the favourite resting spot of a soldier from the Revolutionary War, whose apparition had been reported by multiple visitors.

But it wasn't just these silent contemplations that piqued Lucy's curiosity. At home, in their 18th-century townhouse, Benji's behaviour became even more peculiar. He'd occasionally bark softly at an old portrait of a woman, one that Lucy had inherited from her ancestors. Or he would playfully wag his tail at an empty armchair, as if someone was sitting there, just out of Lucy's sight.

Curiosity piqued, Lucy started researching her home's

history. She discovered that the portrait was of her great-great-great-grandmother, Eleanor. Eleanor was known to have a profound love for animals, particularly dogs, and had a Spaniel remarkably similar to Benji.

One evening, as dusk settled over Savannah, turning the sky a deep shade of purple, Lucy decided to conduct an experiment. She invited a few friends, including Clara, a local medium. With Benji by her side, they sat in her living room, the only light coming from a few candles casting flickering shadows on the walls.

Clara, always in tune with the energies of Savannah, began by sensing the room. As the evening deepened, she turned to Lucy. "There's a presence here," she whispered. "A woman. She's drawn to Benji."

As Clara spoke, Benji, who had been lying quietly, began to wag his tail. He then moved towards the old portrait, sitting down right in front of it, looking up with an affectionate tilt of his head. The room was thick with anticipation.

"She wishes to communicate," Clara continued, her voice a mere breath. "She misses the companionship of her own Spaniel. Benji reminds her of the bond they shared."

The room felt electric. Benji, seemingly understanding the gravity of the moment, turned to look at Lucy, then back at the portrait, letting out a gentle, mournful whine.

As the night wore on, Clara channelled more spirits, each of whom seemed to connect with Benji in a unique way. There was a child who had once lived in the house, laughing as Benji playfully chased his own tail. An old man, perhaps a previous owner, who seemed to find comfort in Benji's presence.

By the time dawn began to break, Lucy, exhausted but enlightened, felt a newfound appreciation for her Spaniel. Benji, with his silent sensitivity, had become a bridge to the past, a medium in his own right.

Word began to spread throughout Savannah about Lucy's sensing Spaniel. Locals and tourists alike would approach them during their walks, hoping that Benji might offer a connection to spirits lingering in the city's historic sites. And more often than not, he did.

For Lucy, Benji became more than just a pet. He was a link to the city's rich tapestry of tales, an ambassador of the spectral realm. Their bond, deepened by the experiences they shared, stood as a testament to the idea that connections, whether in the realm of the living or the departed, are the threads that weave the fabric of our existence.

In a city where the past is never truly gone, where the lines between the tangible and intangible blur, Benji and Lucy found themselves at the intersection of history, mystery, and the undying bond between humans and their faithful companions.

California's Canine Clairvoyant

On the west coast of the United States, where the tectonic plates dance and the earth occasionally rumbles, lived Marissa with her Chihuahua, named Peanut. The two were inseparable since Marissa adopted Peanut from a shelter in Los Angeles. The bustling streets of LA were filled with vibrant life, but what the city also held, deep within its bowels, was a geological volatility that was both a wonder and a potential threat.

Marissa, a geologist by profession, was drawn to LA not just for its sunny weather and sprawling beaches, but also for its seismic activity. It fascinated her how the ground beneath could, at any given moment, express its might. Her apartment, adorned with seismographs and geology charts, also had a special little bed right next to her study desk for Peanut.

While Marissa was keenly aware of the tremors and tectonic movements due to her profession, she began to notice an uncanny pattern with Peanut. The tiny Chihuahua seemed to have a knack for acting peculiar just before seismic activities were registered on her equipment.

At first, it was easy to dismiss. One evening, Peanut began to pace around the apartment, restless and whimpering. His usually bright eyes darted around, and he repeatedly went to the balcony door, scratching it. Thinking he wanted to play, Marissa took him out. But instead of playing, Peanut simply sat on the ground, ears perked up, as if he was listening to something far away. Barely a few minutes later, Marissa's phone buzzed with a notification about a minor tremor detected in the vicinity.

Days turned into weeks, and every time there was a vibration, however minor, Peanut's behaviour would predict it. He would either become restless, hide under the bed, or whine continuously. Marissa found it both fascinating and bewildering. Could her little Chihuahua genuinely be sensing these tremors before her state-of-the-art equipment could?

Determined to understand this better, Marissa started to document Peanut's behaviours. She kept a journal, noting down every odd activity he exhibited and cross-referencing it with seismic data. Over months, the pattern was undeniable. Peanut was not just reacting to the tremors; he was anticipating them.

There was one evening, in particular, that solidified Marissa's belief in Peanut's extraordinary ability. They were at a friend's dinner party in a high-rise apartment. The night was young, laughter echoed, wine glasses clinked, and the city lights shimmered in the distance. But amidst this revelry, Peanut began to act out. He growled softly, his small frame shivering, eyes wide and anxious. He clung to Marissa, refusing to be put down.

Feeling a rush of anxiety herself, Marissa decided to leave

the party early. As she drove back home, her car radio announced an emergency alert—a significant earthquake was expected within the next hour. The warning had been based on new prediction technologies, and evacuations in vulnerable areas had begun.

The quake that night wasn't massive, but it was strong enough to shatter windows and sway the high-rises. Had Marissa stayed back at the party, she would have been amidst the chaos of a panicked evacuation from a tall building.

Days after the quake, Marissa couldn't help but marvel at the turn of events. The city buzzed with stories of close calls and the unexpected quake, but in her heart, she held immense gratitude for Peanut.

She pondered on the possibility that Peanut's heightened senses allowed him to detect the preliminary vibrations or sounds that preceded a quake. Animals, after all, were known to have heightened senses compared to humans. But whatever the science behind it, Marissa now trusted

Peanut's instincts more than ever.

The bond between Marissa and Peanut deepened. They became an inseparable duo, not just as pet and owner but as partners attuned to the earth's rhythms. Marissa would often joke with her colleagues that while they had advanced seismographs, she had a "Canine Clairvoyant."

Peanut's uncanny ability wasn't just a boon for Marissa but became a legend in her apartment complex. Neighbours would keep an eye on Peanut, taking his restlessness as a sign to be alert. While he was no replacement for actual seismic alert systems, the tiny Chihuahua brought a sense of comfort to many around him.

In the sprawling expanse of California, where the earth whispered its secrets through rumbles and shakes, a tiny Chihuahua named Peanut listened closely, bridging the gap between nature's enigma and the heartbeat of the human world.

Glasgow's Greyhound

The city of Glasgow, with its grand architectural structures and historic cobbled streets, carries countless tales from the past. But among its many stories, one resonates with an emotion so profound, it binds the hearts of both man and beast: loyalty.

It all began with a man named Douglas McAllister, a retired postman, who lived in a humble cottage on the outskirts of Glasgow. Having spent his entire life in the service of others, delivering letters and parcels, the time had come for Douglas to live his days in tranquillity. Alone, save for his faithful companion, a sleek and noble Greyhound named Rufus.

The bond between Douglas and Rufus was something locals often spoke of. You'd rarely see one without the other.

Whether it was Douglas tending to his garden with Rufus lounging beside him, or the pair taking their long walks in the Scottish moors, their companionship was evident.

But as nature would have it, the curtain of time falls upon every living soul. One chilly morning, as winter's breath began to blanket Glasgow, Douglas passed away in his sleep. While family and friends mourned the kind-hearted postman, a silent observer mourned the most: Rufus.

At Douglas's funeral, held in the local cemetery, Rufus made his presence known. He sat at a distance, watching as the man he'd known, loved, and lived with was laid to rest. As the last prayers were said, and the attendees began to depart, Rufus approached the fresh grave. He lay down, right on top of the freshly turned soil, his eyes heavy with sorrow.

Family members tried to coax him back to the house. The cold was setting in, and they worried for Rufus's health. But the Greyhound would not be moved. His place was there, beside the man he'd devoted his life to.

News of Rufus's loyalty spread throughout Glasgow. Every day, like clockwork, locals would visit the cemetery, bringing blankets, food, and water for the grieving dog. They'd sit with him, pet him, and share their stories of Douglas, hoping their words might provide some solace. But Rufus, though appreciative of the kindness, never left that grave.

Seasons changed. The harshness of winter gave way to the blossoms of spring, and soon summer's warmth graced Glasgow. Yet, through it all, Rufus remained unmoved. Children would visit, offering their toys and treats. Elderly folks would recount tales of their own pets, hoping to connect with the mourning Greyhound. But his resolve never wavered.

As years went by, Rufus became a symbol of undying loyalty in Glasgow. Tourists visiting the city would often detour to the cemetery to pay their respects to the legendary dog and his departed master. They'd leave flowers, notes, and trinkets, turning Douglas's grave into a beacon of love and remembrance.

Rufus aged, his sleek black coat now peppered with grey, his once nimble gait slower. Still, his spirit remained unbroken. There were many instances when locals found sheltered spots for him to rest during inclement weather or even set up a small kennel beside the grave. But Rufus always chose the same spot, right atop Douglas's resting place.

Then, one fateful morning, a little over four years since Douglas's passing, the cemetery's groundskeeper found Rufus, still as ever, lying atop the grave. He'd passed on, joining his beloved master in the world beyond.

The city mourned once again. Rufus's tale had touched many, teaching them the true essence of loyalty and devotion. A small memorial was set up beside Douglas's grave - a stone carving of a Greyhound, forever watching over its master.

Douglas and Rufus's story became an integral part of Glasgow's folklore. Their tale, one of an unbreakable bond between man and animal, served as a reminder of love's eternal nature. In a bustling city with a rich history, it was the simple, heartrending story of a man and his dog that echoed the loudest, touching souls and teaching generations about the purest form of love and loyalty.

Seattle's Sorrow-Sensing Setter

Seattle, known for its stunning coastline, skyscrapers, and a penchant for the occasional drizzle, is also a city rich in stories and mysteries. And among those tales, the story of an Irish Setter named Bailey stands out—a dog with an uncanny ability to feel the weight of human sorrow.

Bailey's owner, Marion, was a well-respected therapist in downtown Seattle. Her practice was located in a picturesque street lined with cherry blossoms. While Marion had a reputation for helping many find their way out of emotional labyrinths, Bailey, her faithful companion, was known to assist in his own subtle way.

The entrance to Marion's office was adorned with a quaint

sign: "Therapist and Companion". Many a time, clients would wonder about the "companion" aspect until they'd be greeted by Bailey's deep hazel eyes, filled with warmth and understanding. But Bailey was more than just a comforting presence; he had an ability that neither Marion nor anyone could fully understand.

It all began with an incident involving a client named Tara. She was scheduled for her usual session, and as she entered the waiting room, Bailey approached her, nuzzling her hand and resting his head on her lap. Marion noticed the interaction but thought nothing much of it. It was only during the session that Tara revealed her mother had passed away just a week ago. It was a fact she hadn't shared with anyone, let alone Marion or Bailey.

In the subsequent weeks, Marion began to notice a pattern. Bailey would always approach clients who were bearing the weight of recent grief—be it the loss of a family member, a heartbreak, or any profound emotional turmoil. He'd nestle close to them, offering his silent companionship, often even before Marion was made aware of their sorrows.

Like the time when Mr. Everett, a regular, came in. He'd always been reserved, often taking a seat and patiently waiting for his turn. But on one particular visit, Bailey immediately went up to him, resting his head against Mr. Everett's knee. It was only later Marion learned that Everett's son had recently been diagnosed with a terminal illness.

Marion soon began to rely on Bailey's unique gift, allowing him to be present during her therapy sessions. Bailey seemed to know exactly whom to approach, where to sit, and how to be. He'd often place himself beside a grieving individual, offering his warmth, or simply lay down next to their chair, providing silent support. It was as if he could sense their hidden pain, their unvoiced troubles.

One winter morning, a young couple, Sarah and Alex, walked into Marion's office. They sat far apart, the tension palpable. Bailey, instead of approaching one of them as was his norm, lay down right in the middle. As Marion began the session, the floodgates opened. The couple revealed they had recently faced a miscarriage. Bailey's positioning between them seemed symbolic, bridging their shared grief, and offering collective comfort. By the end of the session, Sarah and Alex were not only closer to each other but also found solace in Bailey's quiet understanding.

As the years rolled on, Bailey's reputation grew. Many specifically requested sessions on days Bailey was present. Word spread, and soon people came not just from different parts of Seattle, but from towns and cities beyond. They came bearing tales of loss, heartbreak, and pain, seeking the comforting embrace of the sorrow-sensing Setter.

One memorable client was an elderly lady named Mrs. Lillian. She walked in, her frailty evident, her eyes a reflection of years gone by. Without a word, Bailey approached her, circling around her feet before settling down beside her. Through tears, Mrs. Lillian shared her tale of losing her husband of fifty years. She spoke of memories, of moments, and of a love that time could never erase. Bailey, with every sigh and nuzzle, seemed to acknowledge, understand, and offer solace.

But nature, as it always does, continues its cycle. Bailey began showing signs of age. His movements became less spry, his responses slower. Yet, his ability to sense sorrow remained as keen as ever. Until one fateful day, when after comforting a tearful young man, Bailey lay down and closed his eyes one last time.

The city mourned the loss of its unique therapist. Marion, heartbroken but resilient, placed a plaque in her office. It read: "Bailey - Seattle's Sorrow-Sensing Setter. He listened without words, understood without judgement, and comforted without fail."

While Bailey's physical presence was no more, his legacy lived on. Stories of his compassion, his understanding, and his unique gift became a beacon of hope for many. In a world often filled with noise, Bailey had shown that sometimes, all one needs is silent understanding, a nuzzle, and the comforting presence of a loyal companion.

Apparitions and the Appalachian Akita

The Appalachian Mountains stretch across the eastern side of North America, weaving a tapestry of history, culture, and natural splendour. Deep within its labyrinthine trails, ghost towns and long-forgotten mining sites tell tales of a time gone by. For Nathan, an avid hiker and history enthusiast, these mountains were a refuge, a place to escape the mundane. But on taking his newly adopted Akita, Hiro, for hikes, he started experiencing the mountains in a way he had never imagined.

Nathan had found Hiro at a local animal shelter. With a strong build, thick double-coat, and a stoic demeanour, Hiro had all the traits typical of an Akita. Nathan felt an immediate bond with the dog and knew Hiro would make the perfect hiking companion.

Their first hikes together were uneventful. Hiro proved to be as enthusiastic and tireless as Nathan had hoped. But as they started exploring less-travelled paths, especially those that snaked around abandoned mines and settlements, Hiro's behaviour began to change.

It started subtly. Hiro would occasionally stop and fixate on something in the distance, his ears perked up, body rigid. Nathan would follow his gaze, but all he'd see were trees swaying gently or perhaps the rustling of leaves. Brushing it off as Hiro being alert to wildlife, Nathan continued on.

However, one day, as they were hiking near an old, dilapidated mining site, Hiro suddenly became extremely agitated. Whining and pacing back and forth, he refused to go any further. Nathan, puzzled, tried to coax him forward, but Hiro planted his feet firmly and began to growl softly, staring intently at an entrance of one of the long-abandoned mines.

Curiosity piqued, Nathan decided to investigate. As he approached, he felt a noticeable drop in temperature. The entrance, overgrown with moss and vines, had an eerie, unwelcoming vibe. A slight breeze emanated from within, carrying with it the faintest hint of a melancholic song. Shivers ran down Nathan's spine. Retracing his steps, he decided it best to continue the hike elsewhere.

Weeks passed, and Nathan, putting the strange occurrence behind, planned another hiking trip. This time, they would trek the path leading to an old settlers' village, long since abandoned. As they approached the area, Hiro again began showing signs of distress. He'd whimper, his tail tucked, and often look back, as if urging Nathan to turn around.

Reaching the heart of the settlement, Nathan could see remnants of what must have been homes, shops, and a community centre. Hiro, usually so fearless, stuck close to Nathan's side, growling at random directions.

And then, just as suddenly, Hiro stopped and began to whimper, staring intently at an old, dilapidated house.

Nathan approached cautiously. The windows were broken, the wooden panels rotting, but on the front door, a faded plaque read "Miner's Respite."

As Nathan read the words, he was engulfed by an overwhelming feeling of sorrow. It was as if the very air around him was thick with grief, regrets, and untold stories of the miners who once called this place home. Hiro, sensing his owner's unease, nudged Nathan gently, pulling him away from the melancholic trance.

Over the next few hikes, a pattern began to emerge. Whenever they ventured near places that had historical significance—particularly those associated with miners or settlers—Hiro would exhibit the same behaviour: growling, whining, and occasionally refusing to move forward.

Intrigued by this, Nathan began researching the history of these places. He discovered tales of mining accidents, of settlers who had vanished without a trace, and of communities that had faced tragedies. Was Hiro sensing the spirits of those long gone? Was he, in his unique way, bridging the gap between the past and the present?

Nathan's hikes transformed from mere physical excursions to spiritual journeys. With Hiro by his side, he began to visit these sites with a new purpose: to pay respects, to acknowledge the stories, and to perhaps, in some small way, offer solace to the spirits that still lingered.

One winter's day, as Nathan and Hiro approached a particularly notorious mine—known to be the site of a tragic accident that had claimed many lives—Hiro suddenly stopped. This time, instead of growling or whining, he sat down and began to howl. It was a deep, mournful sound that echoed through the mountains. And as Nathan listened, he could swear he heard faint echoes responding to Hiro's calls.

Tears streamed down Nathan's face as he realised that Hiro, in his own way, was offering a voice to those who no longer had one. He was acknowledging their presence, their stories, and their unending connection to these mountains.

From that day on, Nathan's hikes became sacred pilgrimages. He'd often sit beside Hiro, listening to the echoes of the past, feeling the weight of histories untold, and finding solace in the knowledge that, through Hiro, these spirits were being acknowledged.

The Appalachian Mountains, with their lush greenery, winding trails, and deep-rooted history, continued to be a place of wonder for many. But for Nathan and Hiro, they became a testament to the enduring bond between the living and the departed, a bond that transcended time, and a bond that reminded them that sometimes, all it takes is a gentle nudge, a mournful howl, or a steadfast gaze to bridge worlds apart.

The Prophetic Pup of Portsmouth

Portsmouth, a vibrant coastal city in the south of England, has always been synonymous with maritime history. From the grandeur of the naval ships docked at the historic dockyards to the bustling energy at the harbour, the sea has been the lifeblood of the city for centuries.

In the heart of Portsmouth's Old Town, with its cobbled streets and centuries-old buildings, lived Amelia Fletcher, a widow in her early sixties. Amelia's family had a long-standing association with the sea. Her ancestors were seafarers, and her late husband, Edward, had been a captain of a merchant vessel. The sea had given her family much, but it had also taken away; Edward had lost his life to a violent storm a decade ago.

While Amelia had learned to find solace in solitude, her only companion in the echoing halls of her house was Captain, a scruffy mixed-breed dog with a mischievous glint in his eye. The townsfolk often joked about how Captain seemed to have every breed from the Terrier to the Labrador in him. He was named in honour of Edward and had been Amelia's shadow ever since Edward's passing.

While Captain's affectionate nature and playful antics were well-known, what made him a subject of whispered conversations and hushed tales in the close-knit community was his uncanny knack for predicting events at sea.

It began subtly. Amelia would often take Captain for walks along the harbour. The dog would watch the ships keenly, sometimes wagging his tail excitedly, and at other times, letting out a low, mournful whine. On one such evening, as they stood watching a cargo ship set sail under a dusky sky, Captain began to bark incessantly, pulling at his leash and trying to run towards the ship. Amelia, taken aback by this unusual behaviour, tried to calm him, but his distress was palpable.

The next morning, the town was abuzz with the news that the very same ship had faced engine trouble a few miles off the coast and had to be towed back. The incident, though alarming, had not led to any casualties, but it left the community stunned. How had Captain sensed the impending trouble?

As weeks turned into months, Captain's predictions grew more frequent and unmistakable. If he barked joyfully at a ship, it was almost guaranteed that the vessel would return with abundant cargo or fish. If he whined or showed signs of distress, it was an ominous sign that the ship would face some form of trouble. The sailors began seeking Captain's reactions before embarking on their voyages. A positive response from him was seen as a blessing, while a negative one would lead them to double-check their equipment and supplies or, at times, even delay their voyage.

The most notable incident that cemented Captain's reputation as the "Prophetic Pup of Portsmouth" occurred on a chilly December morning. A large fishing vessel, 'The Neptune's Pride,' was set to embark on a week-long voyage.

As the crew bustled around making last-minute preparations, Amelia and Captain took their usual spot near the harbour.

The moment Captain set eyes on 'The Neptune's Pride,' he began howling, a deep, haunting sound that echoed across the harbour. The intensity of his reaction sent shivers down the spines of onlookers. The ship's captain, a stout, seasoned sailor named Gilbert, took one look at Captain and decided to delay the voyage.

It was a decision that saved lives.

Two days later, a massive storm hit the coast, the likes of which hadn't been seen in decades. Ships that were out at sea reported harrowing tales of monstrous waves and gusty winds. 'The Neptune's Pride,' safe at the harbour, escaped the wrath of the sea, thanks to Captain's forewarning.

As word spread about this miraculous prediction, Captain became nothing short of a legend in Portsmouth. People from neighbouring towns and even countries came to catch a glimpse of the "seer dog." Amelia, while always proud of Captain, was also wary of the attention. She knew, more than anyone else, the weight of the sea's unpredictability. To her, Captain wasn't just a prophetic pup but also a bridge to her past, a connection to Edward.

One evening, as Amelia sat on her porch, watching the sun dip below the horizon, painting the sky with hues of gold and purple, Captain, now older and grayer, rested his head on her lap. As the sea's gentle waves lapped the shore and seagulls danced in the sky, Amelia whispered words of gratitude. For in Captain, she not only had a loyal companion but also a guardian, a beacon of hope in the vast, unpredictable expanse of the sea.

To the world, he was the Prophetic Pup of Portsmouth, a marvel, a mystery. But to Amelia, he was family, a reminder that even in the most unpredictable storms, there always shines a ray of hope, a beacon guiding one home.

Denver's Dreaming Dalmatian

Anna Nolan was a psychologist by profession and lived in the bustling heart of Denver. Like most psychologists, Anna was intrigued by dreams – the ephemeral, fleeting images and stories that our minds weave during the quiet hours of the night. She often discussed and analysed her patient's dreams in her cosy office, surrounded by shelves of books and softly lit lamps.

But while Anna's interest in dreams was largely professional, a series of personal experiences turned her fascination into wonder, and at the centre of this wonder was her beloved Dalmatian, Pongo.

Pongo was a striking dog, not just because of his signature

spotted coat, but because of his thoughtful eyes that seemed to hold secrets of their own. Anna had adopted him as a puppy, and the bond they shared was profound.

The first inkling of Pongo's unique ability came on a seemingly ordinary morning. Anna had woken up from a vivid dream where she had been chasing a butterfly in a vast meadow, only to find herself on the edge of a cliff. The fear had jolted her awake.

Shaking off the remnants of the dream, Anna descended the stairs to find Pongo in the living room. The scene she encountered was puzzling. Pongo was darting around the room, nose pointed up as if tracking something fluttering in the air. And then, abruptly, he stopped at the large bay window, standing on his hind legs, front paws against the glass pane, staring intently outside, mimicking the exact end of Anna's dream.

She initially dismissed it as a mere coincidence, chuckling at the whimsical idea that Pongo could somehow 'see' her dream. But then, it happened again.

Anna dreamt of a beach where she built sandcastles, the waves gently lapping at her feet. That morning, she found Pongo digging fervently at the potted plants, sending soil flying everywhere. Once he was done, he sat back and looked at his 'creation' with pride.

More instances followed. Whenever Anna had a particularly vivid dream – be it dancing in the rain, being trapped in a maze, or floating in space – she would find Pongo reenacting scenes from it. If she dreamt of rain, Pongo would twirl and dance in the garden, head tilted up. If she felt trapped in a dream, she'd find Pongo pacing restlessly in a confined space in the house. A dream of floating had Pongo bouncing playfully on his hind legs as if trying to take off.

Anna's intrigue grew. As a scientist, she yearned for explanations. Could Pongo be picking up on her movements during sleep and mimicking them? Was it a heightened form of empathy? Or was there something deeper, a mysterious link between the realm of dreams and the consciousness of her dog?

Anna began to maintain a dream journal, diligently noting down every dream she could recall upon waking. Next to her descriptions, she began recording Pongo's behaviour each morning. Over time, patterns emerged. While Pongo didn't reenact every dream, the ones he did seemed to be the dreams that evoked the strongest emotional responses from Anna – be it fear, joy, sadness, or exhilaration.

Word spread in Anna's close-knit circle about her 'dreaming Dalmatian.' Friends and family were intrigued, some even slightly wary of Pongo's uncanny ability. But to Anna, Pongo's actions were not a spectacle but a window into understanding the profound connection humans shared with their pets. She wondered if, in the dead of the night, the boundaries between her mind and Pongo's consciousness blurred, allowing him a glimpse into her dream world.

One night, after a particularly exhausting day at work, Anna had a distressing dream. She was back in her childhood home, the rooms echoing with voices of people she had lost over the years. She could hear her late mother's lullaby, her father's laughter, and the chatter of her grandmother. Tears streamed down her face in the dream, the weight of loss pressing down on her.

When she awoke, eyes moist with tears, she found Pongo by her side, his head resting on her lap, looking up at her with an expression so full of understanding and empathy, it took her breath away. He didn't reenact anything that morning, but his presence, his warmth was more comforting than any dream reenactment.

In the weeks and months that followed, Anna continued her observations, her journal growing thicker. While she never found a scientific explanation for Pongo's unique connection to her dreams, she realised that some mysteries were best left unexplained. Perhaps it was the universe's way of showing that love, connection, and understanding transcended the logical and ventured into the magical.

Anna and Pongo's mornings became a dance of dreams and reality, of the spoken and the unspoken, of the psychologist and her dog who, in his own silent way, delved deeper into the human psyche than any therapy session ever could.

Their story became a testament to the unbreakable bond between a pet and its owner, reminding everyone who heard it that love has its own language, one that doesn't always need words, sometimes just a shared dream.

London's Lassie

The bustling city of London, with its iconic landmarks and crowded streets, was home to millions, and among them was Clara Belmont, a retired nurse, and her collie, Lassie. Clara had seen her fair share of accidents and emergencies during her years of service, and she had always valued the importance of timely intervention. But never did she imagine that her own dog would come to embody that very principle.

Clara had adopted Lassie as a rescue dog when she was just a pup. Their bond was instantaneous, and in their time together, Lassie proved to be an intelligent and astute companion. However, the true extent of Lassie's unique abilities began to unravel in ways Clara hadn't foreseen.

The first incident occurred during one of their daily walks

in Hyde Park. As Clara sat on a bench, enjoying the scenery, Lassie suddenly became restless. Her ears perked up, and she stared intensely at a man jogging along the Serpentine. Without warning, Lassie bolted towards him, barking insistently. The man, startled, came to a sudden halt, just as a cyclist, who had lost control, whizzed past, narrowly missing him. Had he taken one more step, the collision would have been inevitable.

The man, initially annoyed by Lassie's interference, soon realised her intentions and gratefully patted her, thanking her for the unexpected save. Clara, though proud of Lassie, brushed it off as a lucky coincidence.

However, as weeks turned into months, Lassie's interventions grew more frequent and unmistakably precise. Whether it was pulling back a child about to run onto the street in the face of an oncoming car or alerting a woman to a hot coffee spill at a café before it could scald her, Lassie's uncanny ability to predict and prevent accidents became impossible to ignore.

Soon, Clara and Lassie became well-known figures in their neighbourhood. Lassie's reputation grew, and many began to affectionately refer to her as "London's Lassie", a guardian angel in the form of a collie.

In one of the most remarkable instances, during a visit to the Tower Bridge, Lassie suddenly began to tug at Clara's coat, leading her towards a group of tourists. Clara followed, albeit a bit reluctantly, unsure of Lassie's intent. Among the crowd, Lassie zoned in on a young woman, barking softly but urgently at her. The woman, initially startled, noticed that her shoelaces had come undone, dangerously close to the edge of the bridge. Gratefully, she knelt to tie them, avoiding a potential slip.

As much as these incidents warmed Clara's heart and reinforced her bond with Lassie, they also brought forth many questions. Was Lassie truly psychic, or was it a heightened form of intuition? Clara was well-versed with the tales of Lassie from movies and TV shows, where the dog would often save the day, but her Lassie's real-world feats seemed straight out of fiction.

It wasn't until an evening at a local pub that Clara received some semblance of an answer. A casual chat with an animal behaviourist visiting from Scotland enlightened her. The behaviourist, intrigued by Lassie's tales, posited that some animals, especially dogs, have an elevated sense of perception. They can pick up on minute changes in their environment - a twitch of a muscle, a slight imbalance in stance, or even the hum of a malfunctioning machinery. This heightened sensitivity, combined with their innate desire to protect and assist, could lead to them acting as precursors to potential hazards.

Though the explanation provided some clarity, Clara knew that there was more to Lassie's actions than just heightened perception. The emotional bond they shared, the trust Lassie placed in her decisions, and the almost supernatural alignment of their thoughts and actions transcended the realms of science and ventured into the territory of the inexplicable.

As the years passed, the tales of "London's Lassie" only grew. Clara would often jest that Lassie had saved more lives in London than she had during her years as a nurse. The duo continued their daily routines, bringing safety, smiles, and a touch of magic to the streets of London.

In the grand tapestry of the city's tales, among stories of monarchs, wars, and revolutions, the story of a retired nurse and her psychic collie carved a niche of its own. A testament to the boundless realms of intuition, the unspoken language of love, and the miracles that unfold when the two intertwine. The tale of London's Lassie became an urban legend, whispered in alleys, sung in lullabies, and cherished in hearts, a beacon of hope and wonder in a city that never sleeps.

The Boxer of San Francisco

In the midst of San Francisco's renowned foggy backdrop, against the towering glory of the Golden Gate Bridge, walked Hayden and his Boxer, Max. A retired firefighter, Hayden had seen the best and worst of humanity. His bond with Max was forged through shared experiences, a solace from the demands of a job that had shown him both heartwarming rescues and tragic losses.

Hayden lived a stone's throw away from the bridge. The scenic view from his living room window served as both a reminder of the city's unparalleled beauty and, occasionally, its haunting tragedies. Over the years, the bridge had witnessed countless tales of lost souls seeking solace in the icy waters below.

It was during one of their routine morning walks along the

bridge's pedestrian path that Hayden first noticed a change in Max's behaviour. The Boxer, usually engrossed in the sights and sounds of the bay, stopped abruptly. His ears perked, and his gaze fixed intently on a lone figure standing precariously close to the edge. Without hesitation, Max pulled Hayden towards the individual, his whines echoing the urgency of the situation.

Hayden approached, his firefighter instincts kicking in. With calming words and a gentle demeanour, he engaged the individual, a young man named Leo, in conversation. As they talked, Max sat by Leo's side, a comforting presence, occasionally nuzzling his hand. After what felt like hours, Leo, with tears in his eyes, stepped away from the edge, holding onto Max as if he was the only tether to life.

This event, while deeply moving, could have been dismissed as a singular act of canine empathy. However, as the days turned into weeks, and weeks into months, a pattern emerged. Every time Max exhibited the same restless behaviour, Hayden would invariably find someone on the brink, battling inner demons and contemplating the unthinkable.

Over time, Hayden began to rely on Max's uncanny ability to sense distress. The duo's presence on the bridge became more frequent, their walks turning into vigilant patrols. Word spread among the locals about a retired firefighter and his Boxer, guardian angels watching over the bridge's vulnerable souls.

One memorable rescue involved an elderly woman named Ruth. Max, in his signature style, had alerted Hayden to her frail form, standing by the railing and looking longingly into the abyss. As Hayden approached, he learned that Ruth had recently lost her husband and felt overwhelmed with grief. The solitude and memories became too much for her to bear. However, in that moment of despair, Max's insistent nudges and licks, and Hayden's comforting words, provided a glimmer of hope. Ruth decided against her drastic decision, choosing instead to seek help and counselling.

As months turned into years, Max's reputation grew, but it was never about the fame for Hayden. Instead, it was the quiet moments, the whispered thank yous, the tearful hugs, and the knowledge that they had made a difference. Each saved life became a testament to the unique bond between man and dog, a synergy that transcended words.

However, life, as Hayden well knew, was not always predictable. One fateful day, as the duo patrolled the bridge, Max suddenly became agitated, pulling Hayden with an urgency he had never seen before. Following his lead, Hayden was led to a man, Tom, standing at the edge. Unlike the others, Tom was not alone. A crowd had gathered, and murmurs of concern filled the air. With gentle words and Max's comforting presence, Hayden was able to connect with Tom, eventually convincing him to step back from the edge.

It was later revealed that Tom, ironically, was a therapist who had dedicated his life to helping others find hope in their darkest moments. Yet, in a twist of fate, he found himself overwhelmed by personal tragedies. It was the combined efforts of Hayden and Max that made Tom realise the very essence of what he preached - that there was always hope, even in the darkest hour.

Hayden and Max continued their vigil on the Golden Gate Bridge, ensuring that those in despair found a lifeline when they needed it most. In Max, Hayden found not just a pet but a partner, a beacon of hope, and a testament to the idea that sometimes, our four-legged friends understand the human soul more profoundly than we realise.

As the sun set on the San Francisco horizon, casting a golden hue on the city's most iconic landmark, one could often see the silhouette of a man and his Boxer, walking side by side, guardians of hope in a world often clouded by despair.

Miami's Mourning Maltese

The sultry air of Miami, dense with the aroma of the ocean, wrapped around the beachside house of Nina. In the quiet corner of her living room, an ornate picture frame held a photograph of her late fiancé, Robert, his smiling eyes forever frozen in that moment. On a cushion beside the photo lay Nina's Maltese, Snow, his fluffy white fur contrasting starkly with the dark wooden floor. Every so often, Snow would wake from his slumber, gaze into Robert's picture, and let out a soft whine.

The story of Snow and Nina was not that of a typical owner and pet. Robert had given Snow to Nina as a gift for their fifth anniversary, a tiny bundle of joy that would soon become a centrepiece of their lives. The three of them had shared many memorable moments - from the joyous celebration of birthdays to quiet evenings watching the sunset over the Miami horizon.

But then tragedy struck. Robert was involved in a car accident, one that he didn't survive. The shock of his sudden departure had taken a heavy toll on Nina. Days turned into nights and then back into days, but the gloom in her heart refused to lift. The world outside continued its relentless pace, but for Nina, time had come to a standstill.

Through this period of unspeakable pain, Snow remained Nina's constant companion, mirroring her grief in his own canine way. He would often curl up beside Robert's picture, his big, round eyes searching the frame, perhaps looking for the loving hands that used to play with him.

One balmy evening, as Nina sat on her porch, lost in thoughts of Robert, Snow began acting unusually. He started pacing around the room, occasionally stopping to bark softly at the air. Thinking he wanted to play, Nina tried engaging him with his favourite toys. But Snow seemed disinterested. Instead, he kept returning to a specific corner of the living room, staring intently and wagging his tail.

Curious, Nina approached the spot. There was nothing unusual there, just an old gramophone that once belonged to Robert. He would often play his favourite records on it, dancing around the room with Nina, the music filling their home with laughter and joy.

Suddenly, the gramophone started playing, all on its own. The needle gently touched the vinyl, and a familiar tune began to fill the room - it was Robert's favourite song, the one they had danced to on the night he proposed.

Tears welled up in Nina's eyes, but Snow seemed ecstatic. He pranced around the room, his eyes sparkling with a joy Nina hadn't seen since Robert's passing. As the song continued, Snow approached Nina and nudged her hand, coaxing her to stand up.

Feeling a strange mix of grief and comfort, Nina began swaying to the music. Snow danced around her, his tiny paws tapping the floor in rhythm. For those few minutes, it felt as if Robert was right there with them, holding them close in an ethereal embrace.

The song ended, but the gramophone kept playing, this time, a soft voice echoed through the speakers. It was Robert's voice, a recording he had made for Nina on one of their anniversaries.

"Nina," the voice began, "if you're hearing this, know that I'm always with you. Dance through life, even when the music stops. And remember, our love transcends time."

Overwhelmed with emotion, Nina sank to the floor, tears streaming down her face. Snow cuddled up beside her, licking her tears away, offering silent comfort.

Days turned into weeks, and the raw pain of loss gradually morphed into a gentle melancholy. Every evening, Snow and Nina would sit by the gramophone, listening to Robert's voice, dancing to their favourite tunes, finding solace in the memories they shared.7

While sceptics might dismiss the incident as mere coincidence, for Nina, it was a testament to the power of love. She believed that Robert, in his own way, had reached out from beyond, using Snow as a conduit to communicate with her.

Snow's peculiar behaviour continued in different ways. He'd sometimes sit by the phone just minutes before it rang, or he'd lead Nina to places where she'd discover something significant from her past with Robert.

One day, he brought her an old journal, Robert's journal, from the attic—a journal where he had penned down his dreams, hopes, and love for Nina. It was as if Robert, with the help of Snow, was guiding Nina towards healing, reminding her of their shared memories and the love that would never fade.

Years passed, and while the void left by Robert's departure could never truly be filled, the love and support Snow provided ensured that the wound slowly healed. The two of them became inseparable, sharing a bond that was strengthened by the memories of a love lost yet never forgotten.

As Nina often said to her close friends, "Snow isn't just a pet. He's Robert's gift to me, a bridge between the world we live in and the one beyond. Through Snow, Robert lives on, reminding me every day that love, once forged, can never truly be broken."

In the heart of Miami, amidst the humdrum of city life, stood a house that was a testament to the enduring power of love. A love that transcended the boundaries of life and death, echoing through time in the form of a white Maltese named Snow.

Newcastle's Nighttime Navigator

Newcastle's historic cobbled streets and narrow lanes, shadowed by time-worn brick buildings, often echoed tales of yesteryears. But of all the stories whispered among its residents, the legend of the Nighttime Navigator stood out, wrapped in an aura of mystery and benevolence.

It began on a cold December evening. A thick fog had enveloped the city, reducing visibility to near zero. Streetlights struggled to pierce through the dense mist, and the once-familiar paths seemed like winding mazes. It was on such an evening that Eliza, a college student returning home from the library, found herself disoriented. The landmarks she used to navigate had vanished into the foggy abyss, and a sense of anxiety began to clutch her.

Just as her panic started to peak, a soft whimper caught her attention. Emerging from the fog was the silhouette of a Husky. Its silver-white fur seemed to absorb and reflect the little ambient light, making the dog appear as if it was glowing. Eliza, ever so cautious, hesitated. But the Husky, with kind and clear blue eyes, simply sat down and waited.

Seeing no threat in the dog, Eliza approached, and to her surprise, it began to walk, occasionally turning to ensure she was following. The Husky navigated the fog with an uncanny precision, taking turns and shortcuts that Eliza would never have known. Within minutes, they stood outside her apartment building. She reached into her bag, looking for a treat, but when she looked up, the Husky had vanished into the foggy night.

Eliza's encounter was but the first of many. Over the next few weeks, as winter progressed and brought with it more foggy evenings and snowy nights, several lost souls found their paths illuminated by the mysterious Husky. From elderly Mr. Thompson who had lost his way back from the grocery store to young Amelia, whose car had broken down on an unfamiliar road, the Husky guided them all.

Word of the "Nighttime Navigator" spread, not through news or media, but from one heart to another. The Husky became an urban legend, a guardian angel of sorts, helping the lost and fearful find their way home.

On one particularly snowy night, David, a doctor rushing to the hospital for an emergency, found himself stranded. The snowstorm had rendered his car useless, and the hospital was still a good three miles away. Just when he was about to give up hope, the Husky appeared, leading him through alleyways and lanes, all the way to the hospital entrance. David made it just in time to attend to a critical patient, saving a life that would otherwise have been lost to the storm.

While countless such tales adorned the streets of Newcastle, no one knew where the Husky came from. Attempts to follow him after being guided led only to dead ends or obscured tracks. There were no "Lost Dog" posters, no calls on radio stations. The Husky seemed to belong to the night, and to the city.

Anna, a historian at Newcastle University, developed a fascination for the legend. She began collecting stories, piecing together sightings, and mapping the Husky's routes. In her research, she stumbled upon a tale from the early 1900s, of a miner named Ewan and his loyal Husky, Max. They were known to help lost miners find their way out of collapsed tunnels. The pair was inseparable until one unfortunate day when a cave-in took Ewan's life. Max was found waiting outside the mine every night, come snow or fog, for years until he too passed away. Anna theorised that perhaps the Nighttime Navigator was the spirit of Max, still guiding lost souls in memory of his beloved owner.

Whether born of tragedy or a gift from the universe, the Nighttime Navigator's presence was undeniable. People began leaving out bowls of water and food around the city, tokens of gratitude for the unseen protector. Children crafted tales, drawing pictures of the glowing Husky, and placing them on their windowsills.

Winter soon gave way to spring, and the appearances of the Husky became less frequent. Yet, its legend persisted, passed down from the old to the young. The city had been touched by something magical, and while the fog and snow faded away, the warmth of the Husky's deeds kept Newcastle's heart aglow.

On a clear spring day, as Eliza sat on her balcony sipping tea, she noticed a Husky with a family, playing in the park. Its eyes sparkled with a familiar mischief. Whether it was the Nighttime Navigator or just another dog, Eliza couldn't tell, but she smiled, her heart filled with gratitude.

In the lanes and alleys of Newcastle, if one listens closely, the wind whispers tales of a silver-white Husky, guiding lost souls through the darkest nights. A symbol of hope, resilience, and the timeless bond between humans and their four-legged companions

The Phantom Feeler of Philadelphia

Philadelphia, the cradle of American liberty, is as rich in history as it is in mysteries. Its tree-lined streets, creaking townhouses, and shadowy alleyways are the very canvases on which tales of the American Revolution are painted. But among its stories, one peculiar narrative endures - that of Max, the Mastiff, known far and wide as the Phantom Feeler.

Max was no ordinary dog. A massive Mastiff with a glistening coat of deep brown and a dignified stance, he belonged to Amelia, a historian who had a penchant for restoring and preserving historic homes in the city. Amelia and Max were inseparable. Whether she was peeling back the layers of a historic home's past or reading by the fireside, Max was always by her side, his keen eyes watching over her.

Amelia's latest project was a particularly ambitious one. She'd acquired an 18th-century townhouse once said to have been a meeting spot for revolutionaries. It was nestled deep within the historic district, surrounded by cobbled streets and ancient oaks. The house, while magnificent, bore the weight of the years, its walls whispering tales of battles, secret meetings, and clandestine affairs.

Amelia, with Max by her side, embarked on the restoration journey with enthusiasm. But it wasn't long before she noticed something odd. While the lower floors and the garden were places Max roamed freely, he showed a palpable hesitancy towards the upper levels. Whenever Amelia ascended the staircase, Max would pause, his large frame tense, his eyes fixed on something she couldn't see.

One evening, as Amelia was sifting through old letters she'd discovered in a dusty chest, she heard a low growl. Startled, she found Max standing at the foot of the stairs, his gaze unwaveringly fixed upwards. The growl wasn't threatening, but more inquisitive, as if he were questioning an unseen presence. Curious, Amelia tried to coax him up, but Max wouldn't budge.

Days turned into weeks, and Max's behaviour became even more peculiar. At times, he'd pace around a particular spot, sniffing and whimpering. Other times, he'd bark softly at empty corners, his tail wagging slowly, as if greeting an old friend. The old townhouse, Amelia realised, had secrets that not just the walls, but also Max, seemed privy to.

One day, Amelia made a discovery. Behind a panel in what she presumed to be the study, she found a small room. The air was thick with age, and in the centre stood a table with scattered papers. As she began to peruse them, she realised they were correspondences between revolutionaries. This hidden chamber was a clandestine communications hub.

Max, however, was visibly disturbed by this room. Whenever Amelia tried to bring him close, he'd whine, his ears drooping. One evening, Amelia sat in the chamber, hoping to document the letters. With candlelight flickering, she suddenly felt a chill, a draft that seemed to come out of nowhere. Max, who was outside the door, began to bark frantically. Amelia, sensing his distress, quickly left the room, sealing it shut.

The incidents with Max made Amelia wonder. She delved deeper into the house's history, unearthing tales of spirited debates, covert missions, and even tragic losses that the house had witnessed. It was said that the revolutionaries who once used the house often spoke of a guardian spirit, an entity that protected their secrets and ensured their safety. Perhaps Max, with his heightened senses, could perceive this guardian.

Intrigued by the idea, Amelia contacted a local psychic medium, Clara. A petite woman with piercing blue eyes, Clara was known for her ability to communicate with energies from the past. The very moment she stepped into the townhouse, she was drawn to the hidden chamber. With Max closely following, the two women entered the room.

The atmosphere inside was palpable. Clara, after a few moments of silence, began to speak. She spoke of a young soldier, Samuel, who had been assigned to protect the revolutionaries' secrets. One fateful night, he was fatally wounded, but even in death, his spirit remained, guarding the house and its secrets.

As Clara relayed Samuel's messages, Max's demeanour changed. His previously anxious stance relaxed, and he even ventured into the room, laying down near Clara. It was as if he too was listening, understanding the bond between the past and present.

The session with Clara brought peace not just to Amelia but also to Max. The historian realised that her loyal Mastiff wasn't merely sensing ghostly presences but was connecting with the very essence of the house, its history, and its guardian spirit.

Years passed, and the restored townhouse became a symbol of Philadelphia's historic preservation. Amelia would often conduct tours, with Max leading the way. And while visitors came to hear tales of the revolutionaries and see the house's architectural splendours, it was the legend of Max, the Phantom Feeler, that intrigued them the most.

As for Max, the once anxious guardian of the house now roamed its corridors with pride and affection. For he wasn't just sensing the spirits; he was a bridge between two worlds, ensuring that the tales of old Philadelphia were never forgotten. The massive Mastiff, with his perceptive senses, had truly become a legend in the annals of the city's history, a testimony to the timeless bond between man, animal, and the echoes of the past.

Tales of a Tucson Terrier

In the arid expanse of Tucson, Arizona, where every droplet of water is as precious as gold, there lived a Terrier named Tito. Compact, spry, and with a fur coat that seemed out of place in the sunbaked landscape, Tito was the companion of Luis, an elderly farmer struggling to sustain his small patch of crops amidst a punishing drought.

Luis had lived in Tucson all his life. He'd witnessed the relentless dance of rain and drought, but the last few years had been particularly unforgiving. With the local wells drying up, and the ground turning to hardpan, many of Luis's neighbours had sold their land, moving to places more forgiving. But not Luis. He remained anchored to his ancestral land, hoping, praying, and waiting for a reprieve.

Tito had been a surprise gift from Luis's granddaughter,

Mariana. She'd hoped the pup would provide her grandfather with both company and a distraction from the hardships of the drought. And Tito did just that. He was a ball of energy, chasing after mirages, digging random holes in the parched earth, and keeping Luis entertained with his antics.

However, it was one of Tito's eccentric habits that soon captured Luis's attention. The Terrier had an unusual penchant for digging at very specific spots in the ground. Initially, Luis dismissed it as just another of Tito's playful tendencies. But as the days passed, he began to notice a pattern. Wherever Tito dug, the earth, a few feet down, would be slightly damp.

Intrigued, Luis decided to test a theory. He started to dig deeper into one of Tito's holes, and to his astonishment, after several feet, he hit a small pocket of water. Overjoyed, he decided to dig at another of Tito's chosen spots, and once again, found water.

Word spread quickly among the small community.

Neighbours watched in disbelief as Luis unearthed water in places no one could have imagined. They began to refer to Tito as the "Water Whisperer". And soon, a procession of farmers came knocking, hoping Tito could help them find water on their land too.

With Tito leading the way, Luis started assisting other farms. The Terrier would trot around, occasionally pausing, sniffing, and then, with an excited yelp, start digging. More often than not, his instincts proved right. It was as if Tito could sense the veins of water running deep beneath the scorched earth, like a dowser with a divining rod, but with far more accuracy.

As the months rolled on, Tito's reputation grew. Farms that had been on the brink of ruin were now flourishing, all thanks to the little Terrier's miraculous ability. With the newly discovered water sources, the community began to rebuild, planting drought-resistant crops, and setting up efficient irrigation systems.

Luis, trying to understand Tito's unique talent, consulted

local geologists and hydrologists. They hypothesised that Tito might be sensing subtle changes in the earth's magnetic field caused by underground water. While no concrete scientific explanation was ever reached, it mattered little to the people of Tucson. For them, Tito was nothing short of a saviour.

In the evenings, after a long day of guiding farmers to water, Tito and Luis would sit on their porch, looking out at the rejuvenated landscape. Fields of green stretched as far as the eye could see, and the air was filled with the sound of flowing water and the chirping of birds.

One evening, as the sun painted the sky in hues of orange and purple, Mariana visited. She watched in awe as her grandfather recounted tales of Tito's adventures. Tales of farms saved from ruin, of children splashing in newfound ponds, and of a community bound together by hope and the magic of a little Terrier.

The years went by, and while the droughts still came and went, Tucson was better prepared. And at the heart of their resilience was Tito. His story became the stuff of local legend, passed down from one generation to the next. They spoke of the Terrier who whispered to the waters beneath the earth, who brought hope when all seemed lost.

And so, in the annals of Tucson's history, nestled among tales of cowboys, railroads, and gold rushes, is the heartwarming story of a Terrier named Tito. He wasn't just a pet or a companion; he was the beacon of hope for an entire community. A true testament to the unexpected ways in which nature, in its wisdom, sometimes gifts us miracles when we least expect them.

Virginia's Visionary Vizsla

On the rolling hills of Virginia, within the embrace of the Blue Ridge Mountains, the Morris family resided in a home that had witnessed generations. Their land, a patchwork of farms and woods, was not just their livelihood but their heritage. They shared this space with various animals, but none was as cherished as their Vizsla, named Ember.

With a sleek russet coat that looked like it was forged in fire and eyes that held depths of understanding beyond that of an average canine, Ember was an enigma from the very start. The Morrises had adopted her as a pup, and it didn't take them long to notice her peculiar abilities.

The first incident was minor, so minor in fact that no one really gave it a second thought. Seven-year-old Jamie Morris was playing in the backyard, about to climb a rickety old ladder leading to a treehouse. Ember, who was usually calm, began to whine and bark. She darted forward, positioning herself between Jamie and the ladder, refusing to budge. Moments later, with a creaking groan, the ladder collapsed. It was a close call, and the family credited Ember with saving Jamie from a nasty fall.

It wasn't long before the second incident occurred. Mrs. Morris was in the kitchen, preparing dinner on the stove. She moved to the living room for just a moment, leaving a dish towel a tad too close to the burner. Ember, sensing danger, sprinted into the kitchen, grabbed the towel with her mouth, and pulled it away. When Mrs. Morris returned, she found Ember sitting, the singed towel at her feet, eyes filled with a knowing intensity.

These events, while acknowledged with gratitude, were chalked up to the dog's general intelligence and keen senses. However, as time went on, Ember's interventions grew in frequency and precision.

One winter morning, Mr. Morris was about to head to the

barn in his pickup. The night had been cold, and a thin sheet of black ice covered the ground. As he approached the vehicle, Ember began to growl softly. She then did something she'd never done before: she jumped into the driver's seat, effectively blocking Mr. Morris from getting in. He chuckled, tried to shoo her, but she wouldn't budge. Exasperated, he decided to walk to the barn instead. Halfway there, he found a section of the road where the ice was particularly treacherous. His truck would have surely skidded there, possibly causing a serious accident.

The family began to trust Ember's intuition implicitly. If she showed any sign of unease or took deliberate actions to prevent someone from doing something, they'd stop and reassess. It seemed as though she had a sixth sense for impending accidents.

Word of Ember's prescience spread through the community. Neighbours would occasionally knock, asking if they could borrow Ember for a day, hoping she might spot potential dangers in their homes. She became something of a local legend, the dog with the uncanny ability to sense harm.

As the years flowed on, the Morrises' bond with Ember only deepened. They had countless tales of her interventions: the time she prevented young Jamie from diving into a part of the creek with a hidden undercurrent, the moment she barked insistently, stopping Mrs. Morris from stepping on a venomous snake camouflaged amongst the leaves, and many more.

For the Morris family, Ember wasn't just a pet; she was their guardian, their protector. They often mused about her gift. Some said she was blessed, others that she was simply in tune with the world in ways humans weren't. But for the Morrises, the why didn't matter as much as the profound gratitude they felt.

In her later years, Ember's steps became slower, her eyes cloudier, but her gift never waned. And while she couldn't play as energetically with the Morris children, she watched over them with the same unwavering commitment.

When Ember passed on, she left behind a legacy of saved moments and averted tragedies. The Morris home felt her absence deeply, the silence of her absence echoing louder than any bark ever did. In her memory, they planted a tree on the crest of a hill overlooking their home. A plaque at its base read, "Ember: The light that guided us through potential darkness."

The tale of Virginia's Visionary Vizsla became a staple around campfires and gatherings. While Ember may have departed from the physical realm, her spirit, the stories said, still roamed the hills of Virginia, watching, guiding, and protecting.

And as for the Morris family, they often swear they feel a familiar presence during moments of potential peril, a gentle nudge guiding them away from harm, a testament to the enduring bond between a family and their once-beloved pet.

The West Midlands Whippet

In the heart of the West Midlands, where the landscape bore the brunt of modernity yet clung tight to its roots, lived Eileen Smith, a historian with a penchant for Celtic myths. Living in an ancestral home, she often found solace in unearthing tales buried deep within the land's memory. However, it wasn't a relic or manuscript that unlocked the most profound mysteries for Eileen, but a Whippet named Taffy.

Taffy, with his slender build, glossy coat, and expressive eyes, was different from other dogs. Eileen had adopted him from a rescue centre after feeling an inexplicable connection, an almost magnetic pull towards him. The rescue centre had no information about his origins, but he was named after a legendary Celtic hero.

From the first day he stepped into Eileen's home, peculiar occurrences became a norm. Taffy would often stand in the garden at twilight, eyes fixed on the horizon, as if waiting for something or someone. During these moments, he'd become completely unresponsive to calls or distractions.

On moonlit nights, Taffy's behaviour turned even more enigmatic. He would move to the stone circle near Eileen's home, a relic from ancient Celtic times, and start to circle the stones with a particular rhythm, almost a dance. At times, he would emit soft whines or melodious howls, sounds so ethereal that they seemed out of this world.

Eileen, with her profound knowledge of history and myths, started piecing together a theory. She believed Taffy might be echoing the past, reliving the rituals of the ancient Celts who once inhabited the land.

One evening, as Taffy danced among the stones, Eileen decided to join him. As she did, she felt a gentle vibration under her feet. Closing her eyes, she felt transported to another era. The sounds of the 21st century receded, replaced by the distant beat of tribal drums and the melodic cadence of Celtic chants.

The sensation was surreal but vivid. She imagined Celtic priests in ceremonial robes, performing rituals around the very stone circle Taffy was drawn to. She felt the energy, the reverence, and the power of that distant moment. And then, as quickly as it began, the sensation faded, and she was back in the present, with Taffy looking up at her, eyes filled with a deep understanding.

Eileen began to spend more time with Taffy at the stone circle, hoping to feel more of these historical echoes, and Taffy seemed more than willing to guide her. Every interaction with him became a step deeper into the past, unlocking stories and memories long forgotten.

One evening, as the sun set casting the sky in hues of orange and purple, Taffy led Eileen to a particular stone in the circle. He scratched at its base, prompting her to investigate. Digging a little, her fingers touched something metallic. It was an ancient Celtic pendant, made of bronze and inscribed with intricate patterns, a symbol of protection and guidance.

This pendant seemed to be a key. Wearing it, Eileen's connection to the land's memories deepened. She felt celebrations, rituals, challenges, and moments of love and unity. Through Taffy, she was tapping into the life and times of the Celts who once called the West Midlands home.

However, it wasn't just about the past. Taffy also seemed to bridge the gap between nature and humanity. Eileen would often find him listening intently to the whispering winds, or following the dance of the leaves, as if he understood their language.

One of the most profound experiences came during the festival of Beltane, an ancient Celtic festival celebrating the beginning of summer. Eileen, with the pendant and Taffy beside her, sat in the stone circle as night descended. As the stars shone brightly overhead, the atmosphere grew thick with anticipation.

The earth vibrated gently, and Taffy began his dance among the stones. Eileen felt as if the very essence of the land was alive, celebrating the ancient festival in its unique way. It was as if the memories of the land were being reenacted by nature itself, with Taffy as the conductor.

As dawn approached, the vibrant energy began to wane, leaving behind a world forever transformed for Eileen. Taffy, her guide in these memories, curled up beside her, his role as a conduit between nature and history complete, at least for that moment.

Eileen continued her work as a historian, but her approach was forever changed. With Taffy by her side and the pendant around her neck, she didn't just study history; she felt it. She wrote papers, gave lectures, and shared her experiences, hoping to inspire others to connect deeply with the land and its memories.

As for Taffy, he lived his days as any dog might, playful and loving. But there were moments, especially under the moonlit sky, where he seemed to dance to a rhythm only he could hear, a whisper from ages past.

Afterword

It's not often that an investigator of the unknown gets to merge their passion for the paranormal with an endearing affection for man's best friend. As I sit here, penning the concluding words to "Psychic Dogs: Journeys Beyond the Leash," I find myself reflecting on the surreal, and sometimes eerie, journey this book has taken me on.

The exploration of the paranormal has been a focal point of my life. Ghostly apparitions, chilling whispers in the night, and the inexplicable – they've all beckoned me to understand, to question, and to delve deeper. And I thought I had seen it all, until our four-legged friends decided to toss their collars into the spectral ring. The stories within these pages have given even a seasoned investigator like myself moments of pause, wonder, and occasionally, a shiver down the spine.

I recall, as a young paranormal enthusiast, I was obsessed with spectres, goblins, and things that go bump in the night. But never did I imagine that my journey would intertwine so profoundly with the world of dogs. That shift began with a chance encounter during a field investigation in a remote Scottish village. There, a border collie named Angus seemed to keenly sense what my instruments only faintly picked up. The dog, with his intense gaze, led me to the spectral hotspots, the unseen trails of energies that our human senses often overlook. It was Angus who opened my eyes to the canine connection to the ethereal.

The stories within this book are a testament to the incredible bond between humans and dogs. A bond that, as I've come to understand, transcends the physical realm we exist in. They hear, see, and feel more than we can ever fathom, reaching into dimensions and tapping into energies that many of us can only dream of perceiving.

As we journeyed from the foggy streets of Newcastle to the hauntingly historic homes of Philadelphia, I felt an increasing sense of awe. The dogs in these tales, with their uncanny abilities and innate intuition, aren't just pets; they are silent guardians, bridges to the other side, and perhaps most importantly, loving companions who connect us to realms beyond our understanding.

To the paranormal enthusiasts reading this: these tales have shed light on a unique angle of our field. Dogs, with their heightened senses, might just be the most authentic paranormal detectors we have. Their reactions, devoid of scepticism or bias, offer a raw, unfiltered look into the spectral realm. They challenge our understanding and stretch our beliefs, pushing the boundaries of what we consider 'possible'.

But beyond the eerie encounters and the chill-inducing episodes, there lies a heartwarming core to each story. The bond between dog and owner, intensified in the face of the unknown, underscores the unspoken loyalty and love that these animals provide. To the dog lovers: amidst the spine-tingling narratives, I hope you recognized the unwavering spirit of these incredible creatures. Their dedication, their love, and their ability to sense and protect make them not just pets, but family.

In "Psychic Dogs," we've travelled through chilling ghost stories, felt the warmth of loyalty, and encountered mysteries that baffle explanation. We've seen dogs not just as our faithful companions, but as our guides, our protectors, and our link to worlds we've yet to fully understand.

Yet, as we close this chapter, I wish to leave you with a thought that warms the heart. Beyond their seemingly psychic abilities, at their core, dogs teach us about unconditional love. They don't judge, they don't hold grudges, and they don't fear the unknown as we often do. Instead, they embrace every moment, every adventure – be it of this world or the next – with unbridled enthusiasm and boundless love.

So, the next time your dog stares intently at an empty corner or growls softly at the still night air, remember: they might be sensing more than you know. But also remember the wagging tail, the joyful bark, and the comforting nuzzle.

For in the vast universe of the unknown, there's one thing we can be sure of: the love of a dog is the most genuine, pure thing we'll ever know.

Thank you for joining me on this remarkable journey. May your days be filled with wonder, may you always seek the unknown, and may you always have a furry friend by your side to guide you through it.

In gratitude and wonder,

Lee Brickley.

About the Author

Lee Brickley is an investigator and author with more than 30 titles currently in publication covering a broad range of subjects including true crime, ancient history, the paranormal, and more.

Born in England, Brickley has been a professional writer for more than two decades. He regularly features in the media due to wide interest in his work, and he has made numerous TV appearances.

For more books by this author search "Lee Brickley" on Amazon.

Thank you for purchasing this book and helping to support an independent author! You are amazing! Have a great day!

Printed in Great Britain
by Amazon